ROY M. OSWALD

with Jean Morris Trumbauer

Transforming
RITUALS

daily practices for
changing lives

An Alban Institute Publication

D1414264

Library of Congress Card Number 99-73551
ISBN 1-56699-219-2

CONTENTS

FOREWORD

Last year, as part of the Shalem Institute's 25th anniversary self-reflection, our staff and board spent some time identifying the place of ritual in our many spiritual formation groups. We identified such elements as gathering in a circle and placing a candle and sometimes flowers, icons, or other evocative objects in the middle of the circle; chanting "shalom" and bowing in some groups; setting aside time for silence and sharing; and inviting participants to be present to God in a variety of ways. In the process of that reflection, I became more aware than ever that no individual, group, congregation, or community can be well sustained and developed without shared rituals.

These particular rituals at Shalem connected with the kind of ritual that Roy Oswald says "move people into more deeply surrendered life in God." To me, that surrender is the ultimate hope for all authentic ritual, if we understand "surrender to God" to mean surrender to the truth of our being and community in God, in this moment, in the particular circumstances in which we live. It is these particular circumstances that Roy takes so seriously in this book.

He points out well the enormous and continuous changes through which we live in modern life, and the individual and communal transitions we experience through these changes mean we encounter a constant round of endings, disorienting passage of time that he (following William Bridges) calls "the neutral zone," and new beginnings. Each of these can bring an isolating sense of anxiety, confusion, and uncertainty. The ritualizing of these occasions through symbols and gestures that express what is happening and what we hope for can, as Roy says, assist us to express thoughts, feelings, and meanings too deep for words. Transformation, healing, and communal solidarity can be invoked and brought forward through such ritual occasions.

This book identifies the value of ritual at every level of our lives: personal, familial, congregational, and various levels of the larger community circles in which we live. I think Roy is onto something extremely important, especially amidst the rapidly increased pace of transitions that people experience today. We often take for granted what rituals we do have, and we fail to consider the ways rituals could best be developed to help us through the many transitions and events of our individual and communal lives. The lack of appreciation of rituals' importance has led to the failure to bring them to bear at countless points in our lives where they could help us to manage the transitions of our lives, assisting us and others to go through these transitions with a sense of acceptance, inspiration, divine presence, and communal sharing. In the isolation created by modern individualism, embracing opportunities to enhance fuller community among us through ritual occasions is particularly important.

This book fills a hole in the literature available to help congregations, communities, and individuals to better understand the power and value of rituals in all the major events and transitions of human living, and to translate that understanding into a "ministry of ritual." The chapters ahead offer a host of imaginative and practical suggestions about how to carry out such a ministry related to many concrete occasions of our lives. These pages should be especially valuable for congregational leaders as they come to grips with the broad range of needs for ritualization that goes way beyond the narrow range of ritual occasions in the normal church's life. The congregation, I believe, is better suited than any other institution in our society to take seriously and bring forward the possibilities of ritual. Of all institutions, it is the one most used to marking the importance of transitional times in people's lives, and it is uniquely capable of steadily giving spiritual grounding and communal context to these times. This book gives churches and temples the opportunity to expand their natural base of understanding related to meaningful ritual as well as to expand their ritual practice into a much wider range of possibilities in individual, communal, and public life.

With its many concrete suggestions for ritualizing a great variety of important occasions, I expect that this book will be one of those enduring resources for congregational leaders and individuals that will continue to inform the understanding and practical development of ritual occasions. Reading this book will surely expand the reader's sense of need and imaginative possibilities for the empowering ritual markings that can help turn the scary blur of transitions into a confident-in-God embracing of the mystery of change. Change is a mysterious reality that reflects the divine ordering, disorienting, and reorienting of our lives, on the way to the kingdom of God. Our rituals finally express our trust in this mysterious pilgrimage.

Tilden Edwards
Executive Director
Shalem Institute for Spiritual Formation

INTRODUCTION

One of the major characteristics of the postmodern age is that change is both rapid and broad in scope. It is estimated by futurists that our current knowledge base now doubles every two to three years. As recently as the 1960s, knowledge doubled only every ten years, whereas in the early 16th century, it took a full century for knowledge to increase as much. Many futurists believe that by the year 2055, human knowledge will double every 24 hours.

During the time of Thomas Jefferson, a learned person was one who knew all there was to know. Jefferson himself was not only a politician but an inventor of farm implements, author, and musician. Today a person with a doctorate cannot hope to know all there is to know even about his or her focus of study. I have two nephews who specialize in computer technology, and they tell me they have trouble keeping up with the latest developments in their own field.

My parents, each born just after 1900, also experienced a great deal of change—the advent of automobiles, television, computer technology, and space travel. If someone had told them when they were in their early 30s that we would someday be driving temperature-controlled cars that could easily travel 100 miles per hour and that we would be talking from those cars to other people on cell phones, they would have said, "You are crazy!" Yet you and I, our children and grandchildren will find such changes minuscule by comparison to the change we will encounter in the coming years.

The rate of change today is fueled by many factors—social, technological, and economic. For example, corporations today spend billions on research, knowing that if they are the first ones to build a new technology, the resulting profits will far outstrip their financial investment in the research. The technology they create, in turn, has implications for not only the economic lives of their workers and all who relate to their industry, but also for the personal and social lives of people throughout the world. We are well acquainted, for example, with many of the ways computers affect our daily lives. We watch our children play with complicated computer games as well as do research for school. Their teachers make use of videos and even teleconferencing. Some of us struggle to learn new computer skills now required in our workplaces. Others rejoice that such technology allows them to work from their homes rather than commute to city offices each day. Still others grieve the jobs they lost when they were downsized due to efficiencies attributed to new technology.

New technologies also present us with issues about ethics. Today, aided by the invention of new medicines and complicated medical technology, we not only live longer but we usually live creative and productive lives well into our 70s, 80s, and even 90s. Yet medical advances have also raised new questions about when life begins and should end. Our society wrestles with the ethical implications of using various medical technologies and engaging in some types of medical research.

Things have changed in family life, too. Cell phones or beepers make us much more accessible to our families, friends, and business associates and clients. Yet the same technology has a down side. It often adds stress to our lives, resulting in our having less time truly to nurture relationships and less quiet time and solitude. More than 50 percent of marriages end in divorce, and an even higher percentage of second marriages do. Both parents being employed outside the home brings new economic buying power and a chance for women to develop their talents and contribute in new ways to the larger community. At the same time, the pressures of both parents working outside the home often leads to tired adults who have less quality time to share with their spouses or to play with and nurture their children. Children are forced by the complex issues they face to grow up quickly, yet today young adults often return to their parents' home after a period of living on their own. Young people struggle with the social pressures to use drugs and alcohol and engage in early sexual experiences, and they increasingly fear violence in their schools, a reflection of violence portrayed on television and by other media.

Even the church is changing. No longer is it the central gathering place of the community. Today it competes for time with the workplace, family life, golf, hockey, TV, and shopping. Clericalism and hierarchy in the church are giving way to greater mutuality and greatly expanded roles for the laity. We are even questioning our basic assumptions regarding the roles of the ordained and nonordained. Whereas we once viewed mission as a faraway enterprise, we now increasingly understand that mission starts at our doorstep. People are forsaking traditional religion for an enlivened and more transformative spirituality. We have moved from the church of Christendom to the Post-Christendom Era.[1]

Today people encounter rapid as well as extensive change in their individual, family, workplace, and communal lives. Our entire worldview, in fact, is changing. Our experience as a culture has shifted from incremental change (change of which we were barely aware) to paradigmatic change that transforms the very structure of our thinking and identity.[2] We have moved from the industrial age to the information age. We are beginning to think differently about gender roles, learning, physical and mental healing, power and authority, the earth and the cosmos, and the possibilities for our own lives. We are learning that change—even rapid change—is the norm rather than the exception. Not only does the change in each arena of life have a cumulative effect, it seems to have a exponential effect. We feel inundated, saturated with change—sometimes as if change were a snowball rolling out of control not only in our individual lives but throughout the entire culture. Some of us rejoice; others despair. All of us experience the stress, the strains and pulls, the problems and the new possibilities that change and transition afford us.

Changes always force us into some type of social readjustment, but it sometimes seems we are not through with one major transition before we encounter another nearly as major, and we may have practically quit counting the smaller changes. Many people who feel nearly overwhelmed by change are tempted to escape through television, workaholism and permanent busyness, gadgets, and shopping. Or we get into the blame game—scapegoating people of other cultures, ethnic background, gender, religion, or people with different values. Instead of embracing the world's complexity and diversity, made more evident through increasing global awareness and high-tech communication, we might be tempted to retreat to the good old days, try to turn back the clock, or point the finger at those who are different from us.

Health is one arena in which to observe the impact of rapid, deep, and cumulative change. Thomas Holmes and Richard Rahe discovered in the development and testing of their Holmes/Rahe Social Readjustment Rating Scale that there is a definite correlation between social readjustment and physical illness.[3] Stress is now considered to be the number one killer in North America. The obituaries don't announce that John Doe died of stress; instead, we read that he died of cancer or heart disease. These two diseases alone account for 65 percent of the deaths on this continent. We have vaccines and antibiotics to deal with the diseases many die of elsewhere. In the Western world, we develop stress-related diseases. Some chronic illnesses we live with, and others eventually lead to our untimely deaths. (A colleague recently interviewed a number of professionals—a therapist, career specialist, spiritual director, social service agency vice president, denominational executive, and an internationally known futurist—about the impact of change in our society. She asked if they were concerned about the potentially negative impact of change on the emotional health of people. Each person she interviewed expressed growing concern about people's difficulty in coping with the cumulative effects of the speed and breadth of change today.)

Most people over 40 grew up believing that change would be the exception in their lives. They have discovered just the opposite. Change is their constant companion. Life is one transition followed quickly by or, more likely, overlapping another. Most individuals and families in North America and the Western world are simultaneously encountering major changes in their workplace, family and friendships, church, and the larger community.

William Bridges' Model of Transitions

Well-known sociologist and anthropologist William Bridges distinguishes between "change" and "transition." In his classic work *Managing Transitions*, he describes "change" as situational and external. We move to a different house, begin a new job, struggle with a deteriorating state of health, or acquire new technological tools at work. "Transitions," on the other hand, are internal psychological processes that "people go through to come to terms with the new situation." External change only really takes hold when internal transitions also occur.[4] That is why, for example, when you introduce some new method or idea in your church, you find resistance and eventually, if ownership or the idea does not become widespread, the church will tend to revert to its previous way of doing things. Transitions always begin with an *ending*, whereas change is about the new situation. Successful psychological transitions (and, I would assert, spiritual transitions) require first letting go of the old reality and the old identity one had before the change took place. We always have to acknowledge a loss: of relationships, familiar patterns of being and doing, the source of our identity, or recognizable landmarks and mileposts.

The second stage of transition, Bridges asserts, is the *neutral zone*—a sort of no-man's-land between the old and new realities. The old ways have disappeared, the previous identity is gone, but the new ways, the new identity has not yet fully emerged or does not yet feel comfortable and familiar. The neutral zone is a time of confusion, doubt, fear, chaos, struggle, and waiting. Bridges calls it an "emotional wilderness," and we often wander there a lot longer than 40 days and 40 nights! Many of us try to escape the neutral zone altogether or rush to push ourselves through it. This neutral zone is a time when we sometimes question our own sanity! Yet it holds so much opportunity and promise for us. Here, if we embrace it, we may find new creativity, growth, and development—even spiritual transformation. Like crisis, the neutral zone is a place of both danger and opportunity.[5]

The final stage of transition is a *new beginning*, but it can only come once endings are acknowledged and the neutral zone has been encountered and worked through. A new situation does not mean a new beginning. Bridges suggests:

> Beginnings involve new understandings, new values, new attitudes, and—most of all—new identities.... Beginnings ... are the final phase of the organic process that I call "transition," and their timing is not measured in the dates written on an implementation schedule. Beginnings follow the timing of the mind and heart.[6]

Although Bridges' work has focused on dealing with the emotional or psychological processes during the endings, neutral zone, and new beginnings involved in transition processes, this book will address the spiritual significance of these processes in transition as well. Change challenges our whole lives. In our willingness to acknowledge loss, our embrace of the wilderness of the neutral zone, and our commitment to new beginnings, we can find possibilities for spiritual transformation. I believe that one of the most helpful ways through difficult transition processes is to use rituals during each of the three stages of transition—the ending, the neutral zone, and the new beginning. These rituals can assist us to express thoughts, feelings, and meanings that are too deep for words—experiences that require symbols and movement to express adequately what is occurring in our lives. The use of ritual does much to relieve the stress of transition times, whether the changes to which we are responding are of our own choosing or are thrust upon us. Ritualizing during life transitions also helps us to mine the meanings of change and transition and find true transformation in them.

Spiritual Transformation

Perhaps it is important here to distinguish between *spiritual growth* and *spiritual transformation*. Spiritual growth involves deepening one's life along a path upon which we have already embarked. For example, we observe many faith rituals in our congregations that continually remind us of who we are or whose we are. As we repeat these rituals, they can move us deeper in our understanding of our spiritual dimension.

Spiritual transformation, on the other hand, involves a radical turning. The Greek word that is usually translated "repentance," *metanoia*, seems to catch the meaning of spiritual transformation. *Metanoia* literally means "to turn around." The term "repentance," however, does not seem to capture fully the meaning of spiritual transformation. In our society, repentance has come to mean inner remorse about something we have done. Spiritual transformation is about more than inner sorrow. When *metanoia* occurs, it is as though we are walking in a certain direction when suddenly the light of some truth knocks us flat. The Damascus road experience of the apostle Paul is a good example of this (Acts 9:1-29). Paul was on the way to Damascus to have more Christians stoned to death when the light of God's truth knocked him off his horse and he lay on the ground, blinded. When he emerged from that ordeal, he was walking in the opposite direction.

Rather than persecuting Christians, Paul became one of the chief ambassadors for Christ.

Metanoia or transformation is hardly a painless process! It normally involves someone or something prying our fingers loose from that to which we are desperately clinging. We must experience the devastating loss of our attachment before we are able to embrace a new truth and a new way of living. As in Bridges' model of transitions, we must acknowledge the real loss and live through the emotional and spiritual chaos, confusion, and struggle of the neutral zone before we are able to fully commit to such a new beginning.

Another dramatic example of spiritual transformation might be seen in a woman who is an alcoholic and then becomes sober. For some time, she denies the fact that she is an alcoholic. During an intervention, those closest to her show up at her home or office and confront her with facts about her alcoholism and the past consequences of her behavior as well as those consequences she can anticipate in the future. It will not be enough for her to go through detoxification to get the alcohol out of her system. In order to remain sober and change her way of thinking and acting, she will likely need to commit to the ritual of attending AA meetings at least once a week to remind herself—in the company of others—that she is an alcoholic and that, though sober, she remains an alcoholic. Without the ritual of going to AA meetings and working a Twelve Step program, it is quite unlikely she will be able to maintain her sobriety. At AA meetings, she will introduce herself by name and add, "I am an alcoholic." Together with others she will read aloud the Twelve Steps and Twelve Traditions, listen as a group member presents a program on one of the steps, and then meet with a small group to discuss living out that step. The process of engaging in rituals of sobriety leads to spiritual transformation. The alcoholic then has an opportunity to continue the process of spiritual growth along the path on which she has embarked.

The Transforming Power of Ritual

Someone once wrote, "It is not that we resist change but that we resist loss."[7] Today most of us have a running list of losses that we may not even be aware we are grieving as well as a number of new beginnings that we may never have acknowledged and celebrated. We may also be struggling with several other messy situations. We are in the constant process of transition. We experience the resulting stresses and strain. How do we capture the possibilities change offers for individual and communal transformation, and reduce the physical, emotional, and spiritual casualties of change? What is the role of our faith communities is this effort? And where and when do we encounter God in our changing lives?

I do not wish simply to provide another treatise on stress management or coping with change. Rituals can do much to relieve the stress of our lives, but even more importantly, rituals have the capacity to help us manage transitions and transform our lives. I want to explore with readers the ways ritual can shape us into the kind of people described in Scripture—more loving, compassionate people, people who are spiritually alive. To be such people, we must be aware of who we are and what we are called to be about today in a rapidly changing culture, one in which change is the main menu item on our daily table.

Change in our individual and communal lives sets the context in which our transformation must occur. Embracing the internal processes of transition from endings through the neutral zone to new beginnings is the route we are called to follow if we would emerge from external change as healthy, whole, and spiritually alive people. When we engage in creative ritual in the process of our working through transitions, ritual has the power to transform us in radical ways. The word "conversion" is not too strong a descriptor for such a radical shift in our identity. I believe that if we within the church wish to be relevant in the 21st century and assist people with the processes of spiritual transformation, then we need to be talking and learning more about the place of ritual in such transformational work. I suggest that we do so in the context of the multitude of changes and resulting transitional processes occurring in three major contexts of our lives: as individuals, families, and friends; as faith communities; and as members of the larger community and culture.

Today, Christian churches tend to rely on members' participation in Sunday worship services or organized Bible studies to bring about spiritual transformation. During the week, relatively few Christians engage in rituals in their homes or communities to ground themselves ever more deeply in their relationship with God. Without such ritualizing of our daily lives, we risk viewing our Monday-through-Saturday life as having little to do with our Sunday spirituality and consequently maintaining only a shallow faith or even endangering our very identity as Christians who follow in the way of Jesus. Ritual experienced in communal worship has much more impact when we engage in corresponding rituals in our homes and daily life. For example, when an adolescent is confirmed at church, that ritual has more meaning if there is also a ritual celebration of the teen's confirmation at home. Prayer and Scripture reading observed in the church has far more transformational effect on us if we enter into prayer and reflection on Scripture during the week.

The major purpose of this book is to encourage and assist congregational leaders to move beyond their concern for Sunday ritual and to begin to envision the roles church leaders might play to assist members to ritualize their everyday lives. I believe such efforts would not only strengthen the spiritual life of those who have been part of the church in the past, but also ensure that those who are newly embracing the Christian faith can truly enter into and remain on a path of spiritual transformation and growth.

A second purpose of this book is to familiarize readers with the breadth and depth of the role of ritual in human life, to help us name and evaluate the rituals we practice as individuals, with our families and friends, in our faith communities, and in the larger culture. I want to draw attention to the ritual patterns that we may have fallen into by default—as individuals and families, as congregations, and as larger communities—and to encourage us to explore what those rituals mean to us. Such naming and evaluating will assist us to be more intentional about our rituals, to keep our rituals from becoming empty and meaningless actions or boring exercises engaged in out of social pressure or for lack of clear options, and to create new rituals that meet our personal and communal needs and hungers for spiritual nourishment. Naming and evaluating can help us value the rituals we have established and to recognize the importance of creating new pathways for spiritual transformation and growth.[8] I wish to encourage individuals, families, congregations, and entire communities intentionally and creatively to design rituals that bring meaning to the changes in our lives, assist us through the stages of internal transition, symbolize the best of our theology and cosmology, and connect us as people who desire to live together in love and compassion on this small planet.

It is my firm belief that if Christians are to learn new ways of ritualizing their daily lives, congregational leaders must assist them.

I propose at least five major roles for congregations to undertake in this respect:

- Teaching members how to ritualize their lives in meaningful ways— particularly in the midst of the ongoing transitions of life;
- Providing ongoing encouragement and support for members who are seeking to add meaningful ritual to their lives;
- Modeling creative and meaningful ritual in the midst of the congregation's own transitions and life;
- Advocating for and leading ritual in the larger community, assisting rural communities, towns, neighborhoods, and cities in their own times of transition;
- Helping individuals and communities design ways to reflect on and evaluate the quality and meaning of their rituals and to avoid potentially destructive rituals.

Reflection Exercises

1. To get a concrete picture of the scope and depth of change in your life, draw a series of concentric circles. Label the inner circle "individual" and succeeding circles "family and friends," "workplace," "profession," "faith community," "neighborhood," and "the culture." Then in each circle, write the changes you are experiencing or have recently experienced. The visual effect of naming all of these changes in the various arenas of you life will quickly demonstrate the breadth, depth, and cumulative nature of change in our ordinary lives today.

2. Recall one or two changes you have encountered in the past year in your personal life, your family, the workplace, your congregation, or the community. Reflect on which stage of the transition process you are now in. Are you in the first stage of acknowledging an *ending* and letting go? Is this the *neutral zone* characterized by confusion, fear, struggle, and waiting for your thoughts and feelings to become clear? Or have you worked through the wilderness of the neutral zone to stand on the brink of a *new beginning*? In what specific ways have you recognized and found ways to honor any of these distinct stages in your transition process?

CHAPTER 1

Ritual and Its Purposes

Rituals can be generally described as patterned activities that create and express meaning through the use of symbols and gestures. Rituals are the most basic of human activities, preceding the development of speech among the earliest humans. In fact, many researchers have noted that even animals engage in activities similar to human ritual.[1] Rituals help us to express more than the cognitive and rational parts of ourselves and are enriched when more of our senses are involved. They allow us to go beyond words. In fact, rituals always make statements about what we believe about life and ourselves, even when we are not fully conscious that they are doing so. They help us express who we are as individuals and the ways we want our lives to unfold (My Story). They express our belonging to a specific family, tribe, ethnic group, nationality, religious tradition, or denomination (Our Story). Finally, they remind us that we live as part of the entire community of humanity who share this earth and that God continues to be present with us (The Story). Each level of ritual helps us express the mysterious side of life, to acknowledge what we cannot explain or fully understand.

The simplest examples of ritual, ones we take entirely for granted, are just part of "the way we do things." These are unconscious, habitual actions such as our routines for getting up in the morning and going to sleep at night. How do you typically drink your morning coffee? Some of us brew a cup at home and drink it while we read the paper; another person pours some coffee into an insulated mug to enjoy while fighting morning traffic or riding the subway; still others stop at a coffee shop and order a latte and a muffin. At night some people lie on the couch in front of the TV, fall asleep, and later groggily stumble to their own bed. Others crawl into bed, listen to music, and read before they turn off the light and fall asleep. Often we are irritated if these typical, repetitive patterns of behavior are disrupted. A friend of mine once said, "Don't mess with my morning routine or I am likely to end up with toothpaste in my hair!" These patterns of behavior—"habits," we might call them— are among our "little rituals."[2]

Our behavior patterns often change when we move from one place to another. Think about two places where you spend time—your city home and your cottage in the woods, for example. Or think about the difference between your patterns at home and while on vacation. Perhaps your rituals on weekdays in the city include rising at the sound of an early alarm, rushing morning breakfast, dashing out your door, and alternating between high-speed driving and sitting in traffic jams on the way to work. There you engage in frantic efforts to do all that needs to be done, drinking coffee at your desk and eating lunch with certain colleagues at a specific time of the day. At night, family members all arrive home at different hours, making it difficult to eat dinner together. Later in the evening, each person focuses on last-minute homework, an unfinished project from the office, or household chores. The day perhaps closes when you collapse in front of the television and finally fall into bed exhausted until the alarm sounds again early the next morning.

Life at the cottage or when you are on vacation might be radically different. Chances are you are not awakened by an alarm clock. You might eat a late breakfast in a leisurely fashion while listening to the sounds of the forest, lake, or ocean. Family members and guests are under no obligation to do anything or be anywhere in particular, so they engage in informal activities when they feel like doing so—fishing, walking on the beach, lying in the sun, reading a book on the porch, taking an afternoon nap. The evening meal is more relaxed. There may be candles on the table and quiet background music. People linger over supper, describing the day's activities or sharing what is going on in their lives. Usually there is more laughter. After supper everyone may pitch in to clean up the table and do the dishes. Later, the family naturally gathers with a bowl of popcorn to play a board game, work on a jigsaw puzzle, engage in a lively game of cards, or even play a game the family itself has created.

Quite likely, we do not deliberately set out to create differing rituals for each location. The rituals evolve on their own. Yet every member of the family could describe, if asked, the pattern of activities at the cottage or vacation place as well as at their home in the city.

We also observe rituals we have deliberately created for special occasions, such as family celebrations, events in our congregations, or cultural holidays. These are closer to what Driver calls the "big rituals."[3] For example, we are used to celebrating our children's birthdays with a decorated cake. Perhaps the room where the party is held is decorated, or party-goers don hats as they gather. Often we make the child's favorite foods and choose presents to give the child. Maybe it is typical for your family to take the child on an outing that day—to the zoo, beach, amusement park, movie, or the local pizza place. And Grandma and Grampa might call long-distance just to talk with their grandchild.

Your congregation, too, might celebrate events such as burning the mortgage, receiving new members, gathering for the annual church picnic, engaging in Rally Day activities, or putting on the children's Christmas pageant.

You will also notice ceremonial rituals in the life of your neighborhood and community—high school and college graduations, bringing flowers to family grave sites on Memorial Day weekend or participating in patriotic ceremonies honoring those lost in war, enjoying fireworks on the Fourth of July, joining other neighborhood churches for ecumenical worship services celebrating Martin Luther King Jr. Day, joining in community Christmas caroling, and gathering for prayer services when tragedy strikes the community.

Such activities are frequently called customs. Sometimes the same holiday has family, congregational, and community dimensions. In the United States, for example, families often travel to spend Thanksgiving together (traffic on the freeway and on airlines is heavy that weekend). A special dinner is served, typically including roast turkey, dressing, yams or mashed potatoes and gravy, cranberries, and pumpkin pie. Prayer at the dinner table will pay special note of what members of the family are thankful for. The family might even participate in an ecumenical Thanksgiving worship service led by neighborhood churches. Children in school will likely have studied about the Pilgrims' first thanksgiving. Neighborhood stores will be decorated with paper turkey cutouts and feature Thanksgiving sales. These customs are not typical in other societies, but in the United States we all can immediately conjure up images, sounds, tastes, and activities—the customs—that surround Thanksgiving in our families, congregations, and the larger community.

Sometimes we also create rituals in order to make sense of and cope with times of transition in our lives. Perhaps, for example, you have engaged in specific rituals when a family pet has died. When my wife Carole and I married, we took on a German Shepherd pup that we called Gretchen. For 11 years, Gretchen was an integral part of our home life. Then when both Carole and I were away from home, a neighbor called to say that our dog had died. Carole and I coped with our grief by observing a closing ritual as we buried Gretchen. We wrapped her in a blanket and together carried her out to the place where I had dug a grave. As we placed her in the grave, we each talked about some of our most memorable moments with Gretchen, especially how she often made us laugh. Once we had finished our Gretchen stories, we closed the blanket over her body and, using our hands, together covered her with dirt. I had constructed a simple wooden covering that could hold a large candle. We kept the candle lit for a few days in Gretchen's honor, and then we bought a seedling spruce tree, which we planted on her grave.

There was no question in either of our minds that we were going to get another big dog. Yet we both acknowledged that we could not do so right away. We needed more time to grieve Gretchen's loss. No dog could replace Gretchen, and we continued to carry the loss of her for six months. Then we went out and found two puppies, crosses between a Chow and a German Shepherd, and we named them Wolf and Bear. We were finally ready to invite these two beautiful creatures into our lives, and we then became attached to them as we had been to Gretchen. After many years, they too died, and we again observed similar rituals. Each time we lose a pet, we engage in a ritual of closure, honor a time of grieving, and then engage in rituals to welcome new pets into the family. These situations call for the creation of rituals to help us acknowledge a loss (an ending); deal with the neutral zone of grieving, sorting out, and healing; and finally make a new beginning. Often we will experience the greatest meaning in rituals that we ourselves have been involved in designing. They fit us.

We might also recall rituals that served a very formational purpose in our lives. Some of these are consciously developed, others we engaged in less consciously; some were constructive forces and some were destructive for our formation. Let me share a couple of illustrations from my own childhood.

Early Family Rituals That Shaped My Life

When I was growing up, my family always began and ended each meal with a prayer. At our evening meal, my father would pick up the Bible and read a portion of Scripture and then an interpretation of that passage. We always closed our time at the table by singing the Doxology together. Only then were we free to leave the table. Similarly, each evening as my mother tucked us into bed, she asked us to recite our prayers. These simple daily practices spoke volumes to me as a child. I learned that there was a God who cared about us and to whom we were to show gratitude. I came to understand that this God listened to our prayers and answered them in one way or another. I could see that my parents believed firmly in this God, prayed daily, and took Scripture seriously and tried to pattern their life after its precepts. All of this became part of who I was long before I ever heard the words "theology" or "cosmology." I believe that I am a Lutheran pastor today because when it came time for me to think about what I wanted to do with my life, Scripture and prayer needed to be a central focus.

Now there were some other rituals in our family life that did not have such a positive effect and that demonstrate the potential shadow side of ritual. Whenever we were out of line, my father would use his razor strap (or my mother, her wooden spoon) to spank us. Whenever my father was present, there was no conversation at our family table. When company was present, we lived by the dictum that children should be seen but not heard. All of this undermined our young self-images and suggested to us that we had little to contribute to the adults or to their conversation.

So you see, there are many kinds of rituals. They can include habits, customs, traditional ceremonies, or new rituals you yourself have created. You will recognize most of these examples of ritual. This book encourages you to name and reflect on the meaning each of your current rituals brings to your life. You will find ideas for how to do this in the discussion questions and activities suggested at the end of this chapter.

The Purpose of Rituals

Rituals serve many purposes in our lives. Some people associate the word "ritual" primarily with religious activities at church, rituals that express our love and worship of God. There we engage our senses in different aspects of worship—enjoying the visual environment of banners, candles, flowers; listening to the organ, guitars, or choir; recognizing the smell of incense; accepting the touch of a member's hand at the sharing of the peace or when greeting a friend; tasting the bread and wine at Eucharist or enjoying coffee and donuts during fellowship time. We are familiar with rituals related to birth (baptism), coming of age (confirmation), marriage, and death. In these rituals we celebrate beginnings and endings. In the Eucharist, we celebrate the presence of the one who assists us in our everyday lives, no matter what we are facing—joy, sorrow, or the messiness of struggle and confusion.

Most of the rituals we observe, however, take place outside the faith community. So pervasive is the role of ritual in our life that to live without ritual would require us to think through every single activity in which we engage throughout our day. In that respect, rituals bring us familiarity, comfort, and a secure, organized routine. Such rituals relieve our stress and free up our energy for more important activities. Similarly, in the larger community, we share rituals that order our society and prevent chaos. We observe red, green, and yellow traffic lights and stop signs. We merge onto freeways in a certain way, sometimes after waiting at metered ramps. We pull over when emergency vehicles need to pass on the streets. We wait for directions from traffic police and alternate with other cars when leaving large sporting events or traveling through construction or heavy trafficked areas. All of these rituals provide a kind of shelter for us—a continuity and sense of security on which we can depend.[4] Another way rituals serve as shelter is by helping us to deal with our anxiety. They help us acknowledge and celebrate what otherwise might be difficult transitions, such as retiring, burying a loved one, or even getting married. Rituals also help us celebrate—as families, faith communities, and societies. Shared traditions and customs bind together our families, congregations, and culture. They help us express Our Story.

We have seen how rituals assist in forming our identity and belief systems even when we are young. Throughout life, rituals continue to deepen our understanding of who we are and who we want to become. They help us to express our uniqueness, our deepest beliefs, and our commitments to ourselves, others, our work, the earth, and God.

Rituals help us heal, too. I have shared the simple example of losing a pet. More important still are rituals that help us heal from the loss of a family member, friend, or colleague or that help us cope with personal suffering and community tragedies. Part of the healing process involves experiencing what Bruce Reed, founder of the Grubb Institute in London, calls "extra-dependence."[5] The healing ritual in which we engage allows us to surrender control for a time and to be nurtured by the ritual itself and by others with whom we celebrate that ritual.

We fairly easily recognize the opportunity for spiritual transformation inherent in major transitions—death, divorce, community tragedy, job loss, illness, war, and the promise of peace. But it is also important to acknowledge and ritualize the other life transitions that sometimes pass almost unnoticed—learning to use new technology, returning from vacation, starting a new endeavor, going back to school, growing older, losing a driver's license or getting one for the first time, rearming and redirecting a life dream, closing a community agency, beginning a new community effort, and so forth.

To be human is to ritualize. God is at work in both the small and the large transitions in our lives and in the little and the big rituals of our lives. We can encounter God in the comforting shelter of familiar rituals, but God always calls us to be more fully human and risk walking previously unknown paths by ritualizing anew—creatively, intentionally, and after having reflected on and evaluated our current rituals. By designing and trying out new rituals, we can better ensure that our rituals are full of life rather than empty shells; that they contribute toward greater wholeness, rather than destroying others and the earth; that they help bring about spiritual transformation—a deeper sense of our relationship with and dependence on the sacred in our lives. Congregations need to encourage and assist members and the larger community to ritualize their daily lives in order to live as Christians who engage fully in today's challenging and changing world.

Ritual Gaps in Our Lives

In a time when rapid and pervasive change is the norm, once treasured and accepted rituals often begin to lose the depth of meaning they once had. We soon can discover that there are many ritual gaps in our lives. I once heard an audiocassette of a speech by Tony Campolo, professor at Eastern Seminary, in which he cautioned that we are losing our sense of ourselves as a nation because we no longer take seriously those national holidays that celebrate our identity as a nation.[6] Memorial Day, for example, becomes the first long weekend when we can get to the beach or open our cottage at the lake. The Fourth of July is just another three-day weekend and break from work. Rarely do we participate in rituals that celebrate the meaning of our basic human rights and the freedom we enjoy or the sacrifices others have made to preserve our democracy.

I recall as a child in Canada, we would always rise and sing the Canadian national anthem in theaters before the movie began. That would not be an acceptable ritual in Canada today. The issue is perhaps not so much that we do not observe exactly the same rituals and ceremonies as in the past, but rather that we have not creatively designed new rituals that celebrate our love of freedom and democracy today. In our public life we have a ritual gap—in part as a result of differences in political points of view, disappointment in and distrust of our public institutions, and changing generational points of view. Some people have rejected the old rituals; others engage in them but find the rituals have lost their basic meaning and become ceremonial shells; still others find deep meaning in such rituals. In our diverse culture, the challenge is to find or create rituals that celebrate our common identity as a people in the midst of our great diversity.

A similar gap sometimes exists in the life of the Christian community. Christmas, Holy Week, and Easter rituals, for example, might be celebrated with familiar symbols and ceremonies. Many Christians, however, no longer understand these symbols, and the ceremonies do not hold the meaning they once did. People go through the motions of rituals they do not really embrace in their hearts and minds, participating because of the expectations of others. Parents might want their children baptized even though they do not understand the baptismal promises they will make nor seriously intend to carry out those promises. They might think of the baptismal service as a nice ceremony or as a custom to which the rest of their family has always adhered. Sometimes these gaps in meaning exist simply because people lack information. Still other people reject the traditional understandings and symbols involved in these rituals and long to discern where they might turn to express their spiritual longings and beliefs.

Our challenges as a Christian community are to bring alive rituals that celebrate our deepest beliefs and relationship to God but do so within the context of the 21st century—not only within Sunday worship and on Christian holy days but also in our daily, Monday-through-Saturday existence as we live through a multitude of transitions in various life arenas. How, for example, does Scripture inform and enrich the ordinary routines and activities of our families? How do I express my deepest pain or find meaning when I lose people close to me or familiar signposts or a lifestyle? How can I face the times of struggle, confusion, and waiting with hope and courage, remaining confident of discerning God's call to the next steps, so that I can embrace a new beginning in some arena of my life?

There is a large gap in the ritual life of congregations. Most leaders are attentive to ritual related to Sunday worship and the liturgical calendar. Assisting members and the larger community to ritualize their daily lives is not even on the mission radar screen of most congregations. Yet when the rituals experienced in the church do not find concomitant expression in our daily lives in our homes and in our shared lives in society, we have to some extent nullified the impact of our Sunday ritual. We experience no congruence between what we say we believe and what we actually practice. Perhaps at no time in the church's history have people needed support for their practice of ritual more than now as we enter the Post-Christendom Era. The Christian life is not practiced by simply attending worship services in our congregation. Practicing the faith is as important as hearing about our faith or saying we believe in some specific doctrine. In this new era when the entire context of our Christian life is changing, the emphasis will increasingly be on a spirituality and ministry of daily life in both its individual and communal dimensions.

Reflection Exercises

1. Take some quiet time alone and make a list of everyday rituals that help you to get through the day. What are your regular weekday routines at home and at work? How do you feel and behave when something interferes with these routines? Discuss your discoveries with your spouse or a close friend. How are their daily rituals the same

as or different from your own? How long have you done things this way? What do your daily routines and habits express about you?

2. With family members over dinner or at a family meeting, discuss your family rituals—the ones you just take for granted as well as any you have created. Try to remember when these rituals began. Who started them? Why do you continue them? Do members of the family agree that these rituals serve them well? Which are your favorites? Which might you want to change? If you like, make a family game of this, drawing pictures of some of your family rituals and asking the other family members to guess what they are!

3. Initiate a conversation with friends from your church or the community regarding the rituals that were observed in your family of origin and in the church or neighborhood in which you grew up. To what extent do your rituals today replicate or diverge from those rituals of your upbringing? Do the rituals you have continued from childhood to adult life continue to express meaning for you? If not, reflect on why you have continued them. To what extent have you resisted or rejected rituals experienced in your childhood or at an earlier point of your adult life? What rituals have you created to replace those earlier rituals? How do experiences with ritual differ among your friends? What might account for these differences?

4. In your journal or with a spouse or close friend, reflect on your participation in the rituals of your religious tradition and of the larger community. What rituals in the religious and public arenas do you find meaningful? Which have you resisted or rejected and why? On what occasions have you created new ritual experiences for yourself or others? What rituals do you long for in your life?

5. Identify other ritual gaps in your own life. For example, do you have meaningful rituals as an individual but not with your spouse, family, or friends? Or do you neglect to take time for individual ritualizing, although you often participate in group ritual? Do most of your spiritual practices focus on Sunday worship, or do you engage in religious ritual during the week in your home or community? What might be a first step toward filling in the ritual gaps in your own life?

CHAPTER 2

The Congregation's Role

Ritual itself is in transition today. So is our view of the church's role in ritual as it functions in our life as individuals, congregations, and wider community. In the following pages we will explore some of these shifts in emphasis and understanding. It is true that the same model of endings, neutral zone, and new beginnings applies to use of ritual itself. As some of our traditional rituals and beliefs about rituals are coming to an end and many are hungering for new experiences with ritual, we are as a people engaged in the middle time of discerning the relationship of the church to ritual in many arenas of our lives. In many cases, we have not yet discovered what shape the new beginnings will take.

Ritual for Individuals and Families

One of the church's key roles in the life of its members has always been to nurture their spiritual well-being. In the early church this nourishment of the spiritual life took place in members' homes as they celebrated the Eucharist and shared their faith together as families and in small communities. Later, as Christians gathered in larger congregations, the rituals of the church were still reenforced in the home by the ritual life of individuals and their families through prayer, Scripture study, and other ritual celebrations of their faith.

For whatever reasons, over time the focus of this spiritual nurture began to have its locus in the church building itself and primarily on Sunday mornings. Parents became responsible only to get their children and themselves to the church so that real spiritual growth could happen there.

At the time of the Reformation, Martin Luther wrote the Small Catechism for parents to use as they taught their children the basics of the faith. But in recent decades, we have taken that catechism out of the parents' hands and placed it in the hands of clergy and other church leaders. The implicit message in this movement is that parents are not equipped adequately to teach their children the precepts of the faith. By implication, neither are they able to carry out meaningful spiritual rituals in their homes. As the result, the congregation on Sunday morning might be rich in ritual activity, although families and individuals rarely observe meaningful spiritual rituals throughout the week.

How did we get to this point? Perhaps no one knows for sure. Possibly we got here with the extension of seminary training and professionalization of our clergy—and later, Christian educators and other church staff. As our clergy and other church staff members became better educated and the expectations for professionalization were emphasized, there may have been a natural tendency for them to see themselves and for others to expect them to be the only true authority on matters of life and faith and the overseers of the spiritual formation of the people. Clearly, it would be most convenient and efficient if this oversight happened in the church building, where clergy would be best able to monitor the delivery of these spiritual services.

In addition, a greater-than-normal discontinuity between generations occurred between the World War II generation and their baby boomer offspring. Many members of the World War II generation did observe religious rituals in their homes. Most of their offspring, however, did not. The reasons are complex. The younger generation witnessed their parents sacrificing greatly as a result of the Great Depression to save rather than spend and often dying soon after retirement, not having experienced the joys of travel or other forms of personal fulfillment and joy. The baby boomers wanted to be free of many of the restraints they observed in their parents; the boomers were going to enjoy life and change the world at the same time.

Meanwhile, economic necessities, new roles outside of the home for women, long commute times between outlying suburbs and downtown city employment, the increase in extracurricular activities for children, and the fascination with television meant that family life styles were changing. Family members were scattered in many directions during the day and into the evening. Rarely did everyone in the family sit down and eat meals at the same time. Praying and reading

Scripture—often associated with family meals and evenings spent together—gradually became less common.

Whatever the complex history of this transition in the locus of spiritual nurture, the reality is that today few people in Christian homes observe religious rituals, either as individuals or as families. I do not suggest that a new emphasis on ritualizing our daily lives will require only a minor adjustment in the ways congregations begin to view their ministry to members. Members have been depending for many years on congregational staff to deliver spiritual nourishment in a central church building, and people might feel betrayed by a change in this regard—as if their psychological contract with the congregation has been broken. Many will likely say, "What are we paying clergy and church staff for anyway?"

Yet there is no question who is most influential in a child's life; all the research points to the importance of parental influence and modeling. Consider the choice between sending your six-year-old child to church to attend six Sunday school sessions on prayer, or calling that child into the living room of your home, lighting a candle, and saying, "Grandpa was just taken to the hospital and is very sick. Let's pray for him." Which do you think would teach the child more about prayer and assist the child in adopting the practice of prayer later in life? I believe that a child's single experience of such prayer with a parent would clearly outweigh many sessions on prayer in a church school class.

If, as I believe, a primary task of the church is to nurture the spiritual life of its members, a familiar passage in Scripture might help point the way:

> Hear, O Israel: The Lord our God, the Lord is one. Love the Lord your God with all your heart and with all your soul and with all your strength. These commandments that I give you today are to be upon your hearts. Impress them on your children. Talk about them when you sit at home and when you walk along the road, when you lie down and when you get up. Tie them as symbols on your hands and bind them on your foreheads. Write on the door frames of your house and on your gates. Deuteronomy 6:4-9

Currently, the majority of families are not nurturing family members' faith or practicing any spiritual rituals. The urge to engage in ritual, however, is both part of the new paradigm of what it means to be church and, in many ways, a return to earlier church practice. Recent statistics gathered by the Search Institute in Minneapolis demonstrate the scope of the challenge before us. Forty-five percent of Evangelical Lutheran Church in America youth see their mother (or stepmother or female guardian) as very religious and only 28 percent view their fathers as very religious. Only 27 percent of ELCA youth report that they have family devotions, prayer, or Bible reading at home. Twenty-nine percent of these youth say they have experienced a family project to help other people. And 27 percent say they have often talked with their mother about faith; a mere 13 percent say they have often talked with their fathers about faith.[1]

Our challenge is to figure out how we as church can turn the home back into the first church for ourselves, youth, and families by shifting responsibility for church leadership and mission. Roland Martinson, professor of pastoral care and counseling at Luther Seminary in St. Paul, Minnesota, points to the heart of the issue: "The church's role is to be equippers of families. What we ought to do is let the kids drop their parents off at church, train the parents, and then send them back into their mission field—their home—to grow as Christians."[2] Peter Benson, president of the Search Institute, adds, "As the family goes, so goes the future of the church. Religious life in the home is more influential than the church."[3]

Ritual in the Congregation

We are familiar with the rhythms and rituals of the liturgical year as well as any given liturgy itself. Today the most notable change in the ritual life of the congregation beyond Sunday worship is the development of nine- to twelve-month catechumenate programs. For many years, Roman Catholic parishes have practiced the exciting, contemporary Rites of Christian Initiation of Adults (RCIA). More recently, Episcopalians, the ELCA, and the United Methodist Church have also developed such rites. Several rituals associated with these programs are usually incorporated into Sunday worship. But RCIA and similar efforts, most congregations are limited in how they ritualize transitions in their own life as a faith community.

Congregations continue to hold groundbreaking ceremonies for new buildings and additions, celebrate the renovation of current facilities, and, of course, engage in the traditional burning of the mortgage. We welcome and say goodbye to new clergy and sometimes other staff members with special services and activities. Congregations hold their annual fall Rally Day activities—sometimes including lively processions around the neighborhood—to celebrate the opening of the church school year and often host a traditional festival to which members of the church and community are invited. But generally congregations do not ritualize most of the transitions that occur in their life together.

Ritual in the Wider Community

The church has long struggled to determine its proper relationship to the world. Even in our own time, we have seen changes in the predominant view. Congregations today seem to be less involved in ritualizing in the public arena than they were in the 1960s and 1970s. In those decades, mainline congregations were often involved in public rituals for civil rights and the peace movement. Today, however, with the exception of the religious right and black churches and their leaders, religious rituals in congregations have become more privatized. Congregations seem to emphasize personal morality and religious practice and the internal concerns of the congregation, rather than witness of the church in the world. I am suggesting that neither the church nor its rituals should be so internally focused. We are called as individuals and as faith communities to be present with and minister to the people and world. The major portion of our ministry begins when we leave the doors of our congregations. I suggest we take our understanding of ritual out to a world hungry for meaning and for hope.

Ministering through Ritual

We are only now beginning to understand that our congregations might assist members and the larger community to deal with change and transition. As we begin to realize the impact of the rapidity and breadth of change on members, congregations themselves, and the larger culture, we also begin to see a new challenge and opportunity for ministry emerging today. With a better understanding of change and transition theory as well as an appreciation for the central role ritual plays for people and the gifts congregations might bring to the ritualizing of our daily lives, we might discern God calling our congregations to exciting new possibilities for framing our mission in the coming years.

But what would such a ministry look like? What roles can a congregation play as members and the community learn to ritualize their lives? In the introduction, I suggested the roles of teaching and coaching, encouraging and supporting, modeling, advocating, and evaluating. We will explore briefly each of these roles, but first church leaders must spend some time reflecting on the role of ritual and the experiences of transition in their own lives.

Preparing to Assist People

In order to ready ourselves to undertake the mission or helping members and the community to ritualize their experience, the first step for congregational leaders is simply to familiarize ourselves with the meaning and opportunities for ritual; acknowledge and reflect on its role in our own lives and in the lives of our members, the congregation, and larger community; and become more knowledgeable about change and the stages of transition. Begin by reflecting on questions such as these:

- How do you understand ritual?
- What significance has ritual had in your life from the time you were a small child?
- How has the role of ritual changed for you over the years?
- How have you used ritual in your ministry in the congregation and in the larger community?
- Do you agree or disagree with the ways in which I have described ritual in this book? Why?
- How have you used ritual to make sense of or move through transition points in your own life?
- How have your church leaders been involved as participants or leaders in ritual in the larger community?
- How do they use ritual in their own ministry?
- How familiar are you with the processes of change and transition? (If you have not read the classic works of William Bridges—

Transitions: Making Sense of Life Changes and *Managing Transitions: Making the Most of Change* [4]—I believe you will find them very helpful resources for your ministry.)

- How do you imagine the world in the coming year and then in the coming decade?
- What changes will you and members of your congregation likely encounter? What possible transitions may you and others encounter that are not now anticipated?
- How will you be called on to minister to and with them during those transitions, and how might you use ritual as part of that ministry?

As church leaders, we need to be alert for members who are experiencing major changes. We tend to know about members who are dealing with severe health problems, the death of a family member, or a divorce. We are often less alert to other kinds of changes—job loss or career change, children leaving home, the loss of life dreams or the need to reframe them. We should be prepared to offer assistance in the form of the ministry of ritual—offering our members ideas for using ritual as they engage in life transitions. Members' transitions are opportunities for them to deepen their relationship with God and others. Such transitions represent *kairos* times when we are called to surrender our lives more deeply to our Creator. Like the ten wise virgins in Scripture, we need to be ready for the transitions in our own lives, in the lives of our members, and in the life of larger community.

God seems to favor those times of upheaval because these are the times when we are most open to being transformed into people of faith. When we live in chaos, we tend to be much more open to the Spirit's invitation to trust God more deeply. The spiritual giants of the past have affirmed nearly unanimously that pain and adversity were their greatest spiritual teachers. They do not tell us to go out and create more chaos in our lives, but they do say that if life hands you a major loss or difficult situation, it might well turn out to be your most profound teacher.

Major transition points in individual and community life are frequently *kairos* times, moments when ritual can make a powerful difference. Such a ritual might be as simple as kneeling and offering a prayer of trust and surrender. Without the ritual, that transition to surrender and faith would not likely be made concrete for the individuals and communities who are experiencing the turmoil. Such rituals anchor the inner decisions of surrender in people's heart and mind. Later they will look back and say that something profound, something they will never forget, happened at that moment.

As church leaders, we should ask ourselves whether we are looking for those kinds of surrender opportunities in the lives of congregants. When we are alert in these situations and suggest and facilitate the use of ritual, we can be powerful catalysts in assisting people to grow in their faith.

Teaching and Coaching

Perhaps the easiest congregational roles to understand are those of teaching about ritual and being available to coach people on how to ritualize the transitions in their lives. Many such teaching opportunities are available in the life of a congregation. The most public ones, liturgy and preaching, will reach the greatest number of members. It is my sense that congregations have not been sufficiently creative in using teaching moments about ritual within the context of worship. Yes, clergy faithfully follow the liturgical year, changing the hymns and the colors of paraments on the pulpit and altar and preaching from the lectionary. They have often failed, however, to capitalize on some of the opportunities to teach about ritual within the worshiping community—to creatively use ritual to highlight, add meaning, and offer spiritual insight to the community's transitions.

Preachers, for example, might be alert as they do their exegesis to the use of ritual in Bible stories. They can look for opportunities to illustrate sermons with stories about ritual. It is important to remember that clergy will not be able to affect congregants' thinking about rituals until they are regularly engaged in ritual themselves. When clergy have experienced ritual as a daily spiritual practice and created rituals for transitions in their own lives, they will easily be able to refer to these experiences in sermons and other teaching situations. Congregants will then know that their pastors not only talk ritual but engage in it because it brings meaning and transformation to them, too.

Dialogue sermons on the topic of ritual can also be helpful. In one or a series of sermons, the homilist might talk with one or more members who have engaged in helpful ritual on both a daily basis as well as through challenging transitions. Each time members talk about the ways they practice their faith through ritualizing, other members of the congregation will likely find themselves reflecting on what rituals might be effective in their own lives. Moreover, on special days of the church— such as the beginning of Advent, Christmas, Epiphany, the beginning of Lent, Palm Sunday, Holy Week, Easter, Pentecost, and the return to ordinary time or the season of Pentecost—the preacher might suggest from the pulpit ways that individuals and families can extend their worship experience by using ritual in their homes. (I will discuss other ways the church can address ritual when I discuss the modeling on page 34.)

Many opportunities to teach about ritual also exist within our Christian education ministry. If a congregation offers an adult education class on the role of ritual, this book can provide background material for presentations by an adult education leader, and the reflection exercises will provide good discussion questions for small groups. This book and others can serve as study guides for groups. *To Dance with God* by Gertrud Mueller Nelson will appeal to those who want practical suggestions about how to use family rituals to follow the church year. Meg Cox's *The Heart of a Family*, although not explicitly a Christian book, does suggest helpful spiritual rites to observe in our homes. For a deeper and more academic look at ritual, read Tom Driver's book *Liberating Rites*.[5]

Your congregation might provide a variety of educational offerings about ritual, including an adult forum that briefly introduces the role of ritual and its potential for spiritual transformation during our life transitions. Some members will be interested in a several-session series. Such sessions might include a presentation, small group sharing, and an experiential portion as well as suggestions for activities in the home or larger community during the week. Start by helping members name the everyday rituals in which they engage—the daily routines and habits they might have taken for granted, family celebrations, or ceremonies and customs for community holidays. Do not underestimate the power of helping others name their experiences of ritual. This naming process helps people to realize that they always ritualize, to reflect on the importance and meaning of the rituals for them, and to creatively use ritual during times of transition in order to find meaning, begin healing, and ultimately experience spiritual transformation.

During congregational classes—to which both members of the congregation and residents of the surrounding community should be invited—adult education leaders can share stories about the value of
ritualizing and encourage members of the group to share rituals they
observe now or that were observed in their families and communities
of origin. Participants can give firsthand accounts of the impact such
rituals have had on them, their families, friends, and the larger community. Those in the class could be encouraged to engage in a shared
daily ritual throughout the course, so that they can reflect together on
the impact this ritual has on their lives. This daily ritual could be as
simple as having each member of the class commit to lighting a candle
and praying for those in the study series and the people and concerns
mentioned in the daily newspaper or on the evening television news.

Class participants might also be invited to take five minutes each
day to sit quietly and repeat the phrase, "I am beloved of God." Group
members might try the body prayer and ritual described in this book,
or do one or both of the following simple chants:

Gentle, loving God,
The mother of my soul,
Hold me as your own.

Thy care and calm, Deep Mystery,
Evermore deeply rooted in thee.[6]

In order to encourage participants to engage in rituals that acknowledge transitions, one class could be devoted to creating a new ritual addressing an ending or new beginning in the congregation or community.
Later in the seminar series, the leader can suggest criteria for evaluating rituals, and group members can discuss and further shape these
criteria. At the end of the seminar, participants should be encouraged
to share a plan for how they intend to change any of their daily rituals or
create new rituals to honor transitions they are experiencing as individuals, a family, or in the larger community. Their goal should be to develop
rituals that move them into a more deeply surrendered life in God.

Any number of other teaching opportunities about ritual abound
in the church: Sunday school classes and vacation Bible school; confirmation programs and sessions with youth or families preparing

themselves or their children for Holy Baptism; orientation sessions for new members; family Bible camps and retreats; or small faith sharing groups. Bible study groups can be encouraged to pay special attention to the stories of ritual in Scripture and to find ways during the week to ritualize lives something they learned from the Scripture study. Social justice groups might teach members how to develop rituals around public issues such as hunger, homelessness, stewardship of the environment, and peacemaking. Print materials such as newsletter articles and booklets as well as church Web sites and even congregationally produced videos can present ideas for ritualizing the transitions in people's home, work, neighborhood, and the global community.

All our teaching will be most effective if we remember that people learn in different ways, and we must design learning events about ritual so that people can use their preferred learning styles. Some people are very reflective. Others learn best through their feelings. Still others prefer an experiential, learn-by-doing approach. The congregation that provides a combination of shorter- and longer-term learning opportunities about ritual, uses formal presentations, small group processes, at-home experiences, and both print and electronic media has a better chance of reaching more members and reenforcing in multiple ways messages about the transformative power of ritual. (We will discuss the impact of personal styles on ritual and methods of evaluating and assessing our rituals in chapter 6.)

Some of our teaching moments come in one-to-one settings and are much like coaching experiences. Perhaps the greatest opportunity for such coaching comes when we visit people in their home or are involved in pastoral care and counseling. Both clergy and lay ministers of the church today are engaged on a regular basis with people in crisis, undergoing change, and struggling to work through loss. Clergy, lay pastoral care staff, and other lay ministers such as Stephen Ministers, BeFrienders, and other home and hospital visitors are on the front lines of those who minister to people in transition—those who are ill or dealing with sickness in their families, grieve a death in the family or face death themselves, adjust to the birth or adoption of a baby, wonder what to do after losing a job, struggle with or prepare for marriage, wrestle at midlife with issues of meaning or postponed or lost dreams, or are getting ready for retirement. These church leaders might also be called on to assist the entire community at times of natural disaster, violent death, and other community losses. We must be attentive to the many opportunities for using ritual as a primary tool of ministry and develop skills to assist both members and the larger community with such ritualizing.

Those who do pastoral care ministry in the name of the church should be appropriately trained for such sensitive interactions with people and should be well versed in the feelings and rhythms of the transition process. An understanding of ritual and how to creatively introduce ritual with people should be part of the training of our pastoral care ministers. Whether we offer pastoral care ministry in our office, at a hospital bedside, in a nursing home, in people's homes, or even over the phone, we can offer ideas for ritualizing specific kinds of transitions. It will be easier, no doubt, for us to see the opportunities when people face endings and the initial stages of loss. We will also need to become adept at assisting people with the long periods of confusion, fear, reframing, and waiting in their lives. Perhaps the neutral zone is where we experience the greatest ritual gap of all. And we should not forget to remind people to celebrate new beginnings through ritual—finding a new job, returning to health, completing a year of sobriety, or committing to a new life dream.

In all of these transition situations, as well as in the daily ordinariness of life, we must both understand and experience ritual so that we can be credible as we witness to and equip those with whom we minister. What a wonderful experience as a church member to be asked by the pastoral care provider, "Have you thought of engaging in a ritual to show respect for this time of loss?" "Have you considered the value of engaging in a ritual that honors your time of waiting and struggle?" "What are some ways you might truly celebrate this new beginning in your life?" The minister of pastoral care should then be prepared with possible rituals, or better yet, take the time to help people develop their own rituals. (A list of suggested questions to ask when designing a ritual is included in appendix B on page 132.)

Coaching is also possible during sessions with couples preparing for marriage or families in initial counseling situations, mentoring relationships, or ministry-in-daily-life programs that address parenting, job transition, and the like. And we should not forget opportunities to teach and coach as we lead and participate in small ministry groups and committees in the church as well as in the larger community during times of transition.

Encouraging and Supporting

Of course, any teaching and coaching also provides opportunities for supporting and encouraging members of the church and community in the use of ritual. But there are other ways to express support for ritualizing our daily lives. We might first ask, who especially need encouragement?

Those who are just beginning to design rituals for themselves might feel insecure. They might think of ritualizing as something only done at church by clergy and staff—something that should be attempted only by experts. They will need our reassurance that ritual and ritualizing is a human activity and does not require professional training or expertise. Illustrations and planning questions for ritualizing (see appendix B) might provide just the assistance and reassurance people need to go ahead.

People involved in the neutral zone—long periods of confusion, fear, depression, hopelessness, or lack of movement—also need special support. All of us find it easier to celebrate new beginnings or even to use ritual to help us through the shock of loss. It is less common to engage in ritual that acknowledges the period we most hate to experience—the in-between times when nothing seems to bring meaning.

Surprisingly enough, a third group of people will especially benefit from our support. These are the members of our congregation who have for some time been creating meaningful rituals for themselves and have tired of waiting for the church to provide assistance. Many members of our churches have increasingly turned to Twelve Step programs, spiritual guides and directors, and small gatherings of friends to provide the spiritual nourishment they do not find in the congregation. Women in particular seem to look outside the church for resources for the spiritual journey. One way to support their experience as creators of meaningful ritual is to encourage them to share their stories, rituals, and experiences. Invite them to talk about what they have learned and to teach you and others.

Gerald Caplan of the Harvard Laboratory of Community Psychiatry once described a support system as a pattern of ties that "validate our personal identity and worth, provide genuine help with the work we are engaged in, and respond to our overall need to be dealt with as a unique individual."[7] As we support and encourage role individuals and communities who seek to ritualize transitions, we might keep this description of support in mind. We validate a person's worth and identity as he or she moves through endings, neutral time, and new beginnings. We provide help with the creative task of ritualizing. And we acknowledge that individuals, families, and communities have different needs and prefer different styles and approaches to ritual.

Modeling

I have already pointed out that clergy and church leaders need to practice what they teach and preach so they can be credible witnesses to the power of ritual to help us discover meaning and bring about spiritual transformation. We need to tell our own stories of ritualizing and share our honest struggles with ritual. Congregations can also model ritualizing. The worship environment provides an excellent place to begin. Because most people, including leaders of congregations, focus on ritual in worship, congregations might make use of the natural bridge between the liturgical calendar of the church and people's transitions in their daily lives. Worship could be a natural place for the church to begin to expand its ministry of ritualizing transitions.

In all of the years that I have been a member of a congregation, it has been the altar guild that changed the paraments on the pulpit, lectern, and altar well before the liturgical season or observance arrives. What would it be like to change those paraments during the worship service itself? This ritual could, in fact, be the sermon for the day! Imagine the last service of the liturgical year, called Christ the King Sunday or Reign of Christ Sunday in some traditions. The service begins with the white paraments in place. At a time appropriate to the congregation's usual worship practice, perhaps before the first lesson is read or before the congregation is dismissed from worship, the worship leader calls attention to the transition taking place that Sunday. First, the congregation acknowledges the white paraments and the ending that is occurring. Members of the worshiping body are invited to reflect on the spiritual good that has happened during those many Sundays of ordinary time after Pentecost, Sundays when the paraments were green. They are asked to call out the names of favorite hymns that were sung in that period of the church year. They mention some of the gains and losses that took place in the congregation since last spring, when the Pentecost season began. Then the worship leader offers a prayer of thanksgiving for the wonders of the past season, acknowledging the losses and sorrow experienced by the congregation during that time. After this brief sharing and prayer, the altar guild (or a family and several single members of the church) come forward and remove the paraments from the altar, lectern, and pulpit. As they carry these paraments to the back of the nave, the faith community sits in silence, reflecting on the bare furnishings before them and waiting.

After a time of silence, the pastor or worship leader talks about the nature of transitions and about this time of anxious waiting before a new beginning can take place. The significance of the white paraments as symbols of our waiting for Christ to return might also be mentioned. In smaller congregations, the pastor could engage the congregation in a dialogue about some of the difficulties people have experienced as they have waited for a new beginning to take place. Those present might even reflect on their own feelings of anxiety about this change in the worship routine, perhaps particularly the bareness and silence. In larger congregations, the worship leader might do a five-minute homily on waiting and conclude with a prayer about trusting God as we wait for new beginnings in our life.

Then the assembly sings the first Advent hymn. During the singing, the altar guild or other designated team enters with new purple or blue paraments (whatever the congregation usually uses during Advent) and dresses the altar, pulpit, and lectern. The acolytes bring in the Advent wreath and light the first candle. Following the hymn, the symbolism of the purple or blue of the paraments and the meaning of the Advent wreath and candles are explained. The leader might also offer a prayer expressing hope for this time of waiting and gratitude for the new beginning we experience in Advent.

The presider could continue the dialogue with the congregation regarding transitions. Thought-provoking questions might include: Are you ready to begin this new Advent season? If so, how are you going to prepare for the coming of Christ at Christmas this year? In what rituals will you engage as individuals, family, friends and neighbors to help you to emphasize the meaning of Advent and avoid being swept up in the commercial side of Christmas preparations? For what experiences do you wait during this Advent season? How do you yearn for the Spirit of God to become incarnate and take on flesh in your life this coming year?

Alternatively, one or two members might offer a brief overview of ways they or their families plan to celebrate Advent in their home.

After the worship service, devotional booklets on transitions and the use of ritual could be distributed to members of the congregation. Members might be invited to an Advent event that addresses life transitions with a particular focus on Advent as a celebration of the neutral time, the time of waiting. During this intergenerational event, members of the church from different life situations and age groups would be invited to share their experiences of waiting and practicing rituals of waiting.

Similarly, a congregation could ritualize the change that takes place from Advent to Christmas, from Easter to Pentecost, and so forth. Each time the Sunday worship service centers on such a transition, members of the church are invited to think more deeply about how they might ritualize the transitions that take place in their individual and family lives, in their neighborhood, and in the world.

Many other opportunities for modeling exist. Chapter 4 deals exclusively with nonliturgical transitions in congregational life. Each time the congregation chooses to ritualize these transitions, it models for members of the congregation the central importance of ritual in spiritual transformation and in helping us move through transitions.

Advocating

As you can tell, I am a real advocate of the role of ritual in bringing about spiritual transformation in the midst of our constantly changing lives as individuals and communities. You can be an advocate, too. In some ways our advocate role captures all the other roles. It includes teaching, supporting and encouraging, modeling, and evaluating (addressed below). We can only be credible witnesses and advocates about things we ourselves practice. Both church leaders and congregations will be more effective advocates for ritualizing in daily life and will themselves deepen spiritually if they practice creative, meaningful ritual each day and during transitions.

Lay leaders and staff members can also be strong advocates for ritualizing the transitions within the life of the congregation. Be alert to opportunities such as the beginning and ending of major congregational campaigns, ministry programs, changing leadership, and so forth. Take the opportunity to build ritual into your regularly scheduled committee and group meetings at the church. Urge colleagues or group members to help design these rituals.

Your congregation and its leaders can become advocates in your community to the extent that you are known as a congregation that takes its own ritual seriously; understands and values change; engages in ritual to make meaning of its own transition processes; and assists its members to ritualize the endings, neutral zones, and new beginnings they experience. With those experiences in mind, you can be advocates for and leaders in using ritual in public life. You will be looked to for advice and ideas when community losses occur, when tragedy strikes, and when the community undertakes exciting new ventures. You might be able to advocate for the use of ritual in the ongoing struggles to create a more just and caring environment in which residents can live and work. Moreover, through your role as advocate and then coach, supporter, and evaluator, you can minister within the larger community in new ways that bring healing, peace, and renewed hope. Many practical ideas for such ritualizing in the public arena will be explored in chapter 5.

The writing of this book follows several months of nationwide reflection on the shooting death of 15 students and teachers at Columbine High School in suburban Denver by two students who also shot themselves to death. The shock and horror of that event led our nation to examine again its schools, media, availability of guns, and cultural values. We asked ourselves what we could have done to prevent such a situation, and churches, of course, were involved in the healing of that community. I imagine several congregations in that community converging around that high school, combining services to hold one worship service in the auditorium of the school. Students at the school and their families join in the community service led by leaders of Christian, Jewish, Moslem, Buddhist, and other religious traditions. The theme of the service is the ongoing conflict in the world between the forces of darkness and the forces of light. The interfaith service is a testimony to reclaiming that school as an ongoing source of light in its community.

After the initial gathering of the assembly and opening prayers and song, service participants divide into smaller groups and spread out to the various rooms throughout the school, including those in which deaths occurred. In each area of the school, someone leads prayers for the redemption of that space, reclaiming the room for the purposes of healing,

learning, growth, and friendship. Participants of different faith traditions first join hands and then collectively extend their hands in blessing over the four corners of the room. The various groups leave these
reclaimed rooms and hallways and sing as they move to join the entire
worshiping community outside. There the assembly processes around
the entire school and sings together, as a way of reclaiming this space
for the sake of community health and healing. The entire interfaith
congregation encircles the building, and people extend their hands
first toward the school building and then outwardly toward the city in
a final blessing of healing and reclamation.

Such rituals will happen in communities where leaders in various congregations understand the transformative power of ritual, advocate for it,
and are ready to serve as resources in planning and leading such ritual.
Providing leadership for ritual seems to me to be among the most meaningful ways the church might minister at critical junctures in the public
life of the broader community. (We will explore many other examples of
public ritual in the community in chapter 5.)

Evaluating

Chapter 6 of this book provides ideas for evaluative criteria that will help
members of the church and community evaluate the quality and meaning
of their rituals. Here we want to look at the opportunities for such evaluation. Teaching some of these evaluation criteria and processes could be
part of any in-depth learning experience for adults. Preachers can also
include such criteria in their sermon illustrations about ritual.

Pastoral care ministers, youth ministers, and those preparing young
people for confirmation have many opportunities to help people reflect on
the meaning, benefits, and spiritual transformation of their current and
potential rituals. In the process of evaluation, ongoing relationships of trust
with members will be especially important, as will our willingness to share
our own experiences with rituals that have not fit us and our personal styles,
formerly meaningful rituals that have become empty shells for us, rituals
in which we have participated only out of a sense of social pressure, or
rituals (perhaps our own) that have even been destructive. The process of
assessing and evaluating personal rituals can be scary for many people.
When church leaders minister with personal vulnerability, they can

help members to avoid feeling ashamed of their own experiences with ritual, better assist them in strengthening the authenticity and meaning of their rituals, and help ensure that their rituals are not harmful to themselves or others.

Groups that do ritual planning to address the transitions in congregational life or who participate in public ritualizing in the larger community should suggest ways of assessing and evaluating our church and public rituals to ensure that they contribute toward community health and wholeness, that they are not exclusive or destructive in any way, and that they remain alive and meaningful. Such processes can be included in planning rituals as well as part of the closure to such ritual activities.

Summary

We have briefly explored several key roles that faith communities might play in assisting individuals, families, the congregation itself, and the larger community to ritualize transitions. These roles are mutually reenforcing and often hard to distinguish from one other. In most cases, church leaders may engage in these roles nearly simultaneously. Consider some of the reflection questions and exercises that follow, and then turn to chapters 3, 4, and 5 for specific rituals for endings, the neutral zones, and new beginnings in three arenas of life: in our personal life, our congregations, and the larger community.

Reflection Exercises

1. Discuss what you believe to be some of the causes for the church having centered its ritual life primarily within the worship life of the congregation rather than emphasizing ritual in our homes and neighborhoods.

2. On a sheet of paper, make several columns and write above each column one of six headings: myself, my family, my friends, my church at worship, other church events and ministries, and my community. Under each heading, list rituals that you have participated

in or know about. Now on a second sheet, draw circles of different sizes to indicate the relative strength of your ritualizing in each arena described by one of the columns on the first sheet. Talk with family members or friends about what you learn from this exercise.

3. In a small group, share one or two of the most memorable rituals in which you have participated in each arena listed in question 2. What made the ritual meaningful for you?

4. As a leader in the church, do your gifts lie in teaching about ritual? coaching? supporting and encouraging? modeling? advocating? evaluating? Where in your ministry do you see opportunities to play these leadership roles involving ritual? How might you begin to extend these leadership roles beyond your current efforts to reach families and the larger community?

CHAPTER 3

Ritualizing as Individuals and Families

Daily Rituals

A primary arena for ritualizing is in our personal lives—as individuals, families, and in small friendship groups. These opportunities for ritualizing come each day of the week. Although our focus in this book is on rituals for transition times, I do want to share a bit about the importance of regular daily and weekly rituals. Such regular rituals deepen our trust and relationship with God, keep us in spiritual, emotional, and physical shape, and prepare us for the inevitable changes in life, some of which will rock us to the core of our identity. We usually think of rituals in the context of relationships with others, whether in the family, congregation, or larger community. Rituals, however, also help us deepen our relationship with ourselves. Individual daily rituals are important both for people who live with others as well as for those who live alone. To engage in Sunday ritual in a worshiping congregation without using ritual and prayer during the rest of our week is to live a severely disjointed life.

Perhaps many readers will lament, "But where in my busy schedule could I find time to observe any daily rituals?" Well, as we discussed in chapter 1, you already do! All of us engage in specific routines during our day. Think of what you typically do the first hour of each day. You will probably discover your pattern of behavior is quite predictable. I invite you to consider now some simple shifts in your daily schedule that in the long run will have a profound effect on your life. Author and sculptor Kent Nerburn writes that "ritual is routine infused with mindfulness. It is habit made holy."[1] My invitation is to a ritual life of greater mindfulness—one of holy intent.

Even our ordinary daily habits can become infused with spiritual attentiveness and intent. When your feet hit the floor in the morning, you might simply say, "Lord, this day is yours—from my morning routines that I am about to begin and throughout my day until my feet are tucked back in this bed. Let me be attentive to each precious moment that is your gift." Believe me, you will find new joy in the simplest activities, including tasting the toothpaste as you brush, drinking sweet water, taking a refreshing shower, readying your children for school, listening to the sound of the birds as you walk to your car or the bus. Greater spiritual meaning in daily ritual is to be found in staying attentive to the present moment

I suggest you introduce other rituals that will remind you of who you are and how you want to live. Quality rituals address our very identity, and out of this identity flow our actions. Because I am *this* person, I act *this* way in *this* particular situation.

Helpful Daily Rituals for Individuals

I find it helpful to engage in simple daily rituals that remind me of my spiritual identity. The gesture of bowing my head before eating a meal reminds me that I am blessed to have ready access to good food and signals to those around me that I am a person who recognizes my dependence on a higher power. Most of us read a daily paper. Placing our hand in a sign of blessing on that paper might indicate our prayer for the issues and concerns reported inside and signify our common human bond with people throughout the world whose lives are discussed in the news. I chant and use affirmations while I drive my car. Others I know use their driving time for intercessory prayers for people or concerns on their prayer list. A colleague of mine often finds herself softly asking God to bless people she sees along her route—an older woman crossing a street, youngsters waiting for a school bus, a driver who cuts in front of her, a group of teenage boys swaggering along the sidewalk, a homeless person slumped on a stoop.

A common daily ritual of many people is rising early in the morning for coffee, prayer, and reflection on Scripture and other readings. Other people journal either in the morning or before they go to bed at night, writing a letter to God, a gratitude list, or affirmations; recording their dreams; reflecting on their daily readings; engaging in dialogue with God or a religious figure; or writing a simple stream of consciousness.

The rituals of physical activity are important, too. Some people engage in reflection and prayer while they walk, run, swim, or do other physical activity, such as working in the garden or mowing the lawn. I have also discovered great value in engaging in a simple body prayer that goes like this:

> I raise my hands to the sky as an act of surrender, symbolically offering my life to God. Then I let my arms slowly float apart, symbolizing my entering into a receptive mode and allowing grace to pour into my life. As my hands reach shoulder height, I bow my head and arms forward, offering myself in love and service to a hurting world. I conclude by once again cupping my hands and lifting my arms up as an offering to God.

I do intercessory prayer in a similar way, raising my arms to symbolically lift the one I pray for into the presence of God, asking for God's unique blessing on this person as I lower my hands and head, and then again, cupping my hands and raising my arms to bring another person to God in prayer.

Other Individual Rituals for Daily Life

• *Conscious eating*: Be attentive to the food you eat and the process of enjoying a meal instead of pulling food out of the cupboard or refrigerator and heading for the television, newspaper, or a book. Set aside a leisurely period for your meal—perhaps lowering the lights and lighting a candle and putting on some soft music. Conscious eating can be a pathway to God, a tangible experience of God through the sense of taste. A kind of miracle takes place as we ingest our food and thereby make another part of God's creation—a plant or animal—part of ourselves. How easy it is to take for granted this miraculous transformation. Attentive eating increases our awareness of God sustaining us as a living body.[2]

• *Contemplative prayer*: This type of prayer, often called apophatic prayer, differs from our typical prayers of gratitude and request. Instead, contemplative prayer involves moving toward silence and waiting and listening for God to speak to us. It is the prayer of Elijah in which God came not in the wind, earthquake, or storm but in the "sound of sheer silence" (1 Kings 19:12). To help you stay focused on God during this silence, repeat in time with your breath a sacred word or phrase that triggers for you images of God. You might repeat, "Kyrie eleison; Lord, have mercy," or "Be still and know that I am God," or simply "Oh, God." You will find twenty minutes of such prayer will bring greater calm to your entire day, make you more attentive to all that happens around you, and probably lower your blood pressure!

• *Movement meditation*:[3] Take time to stretch all of the muscles of your body each day. This entire routine takes about twenty minutes. You might think of yourself as "dancing before the Lord" as King David did. Such stretching will also remind you that you are an incarnate being—a body. Teilhard de Chardin once wrote, "We are not physical beings having a spiritual experience. We are spiritual beings having a physical experience."[4] Alternatively, other body meditations might include crawling into a hot tub on a cold winter day or into a cool pool of water on a sizzling summer afternoon. These rituals will help you remember that your entire being is totally surrounded by the love of God, that God's love is so hot we can hardly stand it, or that God's love is soothingly cool when we need to feel quiet and centered. Allow yourself to luxuriate in these experiences and become transformed into a new, loving person.

• *Waiting in traffic*: When you are stuck in heavy traffic, instead of listening to the radio, tape, or CD, or complaining about traffic tie-ups—all of which may very well make you more tense—try chanting or singing a familiar hymn. Such a ritual has a double impact. The words combined with a melody focus and calm us in the moment and are also likely to come back to us later. (When the chant or song does return to you, you might ask your unconscious, "Why are you giving me this song at this time?") I caution you to choose your chants wisely, because repeating them frequently will tend to shape your identity and your life. Choose words that remind you of your relationship to the Holy Mysterious One who dwells with you always and constantly calls you to relationship.[5]

Meal Rituals for Families

We all know the challenges today of gathering the entire family at home. As I noted in chapter 1, I believe that making a commitment to eat several meals together during the week will greatly enrich family life. When you come together to share a meal, begin and end that meal with a ritual. A simple grace, whether said or sung, familiar or unique and spontaneous, will have longtime effects on members of the family. But you might try other rituals before the meal as well. One family created its own meal ritual by taking a tiny bit of food from each serving dish and placing it in the center of the table on a saucer with a lighted candle. The family then held hands around the table while standing and singing a blessing. It was their symbolic gesture that all the food they consumed that evening was, indeed, blessed.

One of my favorite concluding rituals to a meal is singing together. A family might choose several favorite simple songs and take turns deciding which to sing as a close to their meal. Singing in unison symbolizes our unity. You can actually feel the shared energy among you. I believe such singing has a tremendous staying power on our unconscious. Each family has a unique sound, and when a family member is away, it will be obvious that an important voice is missing. Such music should be chosen carefully. The words should reflect sound theology and deep meaning. Our music has character-shaping potential; it affects our very identity. Perhaps rather than choosing a familiar hymn such as the doxology, a family might pick the first verse of a hymn that has unique meaning for them. Later, family members might add another song or two.

Ritualizing the Comings and Goings of Family Members

One of the daily transitions we hardly notice is the coming and going of family members. Children leave for school or play; Mom and Dad leave for work or meetings or out-of-town business. Later in this chapter I will suggest some rituals for longer separations, but here are some brief suggestions for the more routine departures and arrivals of family members.

We communicate our love and care of family members when we take time to acknowledge that they are leaving or returning to home.

Typically we hug or kiss each other hello and goodbye. The family of a colleague of mine always gathers at the door to wish family members goodbye—which is quite a ritual, because there are seven members in their family!

In another family, the parents make the sign of the cross on each child's heads at bedtime. Those children are now teenagers and are leaving for school about the time their father comes down to breakfast in his bathrobe. Before the teens leave they say to their dad, "C'mon, Dad, do me. I need to get to school." What was once a bedtime ritual has a new place in the rhythm of the day. The teens insist their father make the sign on the cross on their upper body and then give them a hug. These young people would not think of leaving their home without their father's traditional blessing. Each day, this morning ritual reminds them of their father's love and their baptism.

A Powerful Weekly Ritual

Imagine what it might feel like to take a day each week and spend it in pure restfulness. I do not mean a typical day off during which you catch up on cleaning the house, running errands, or finishing the yard work. Rather, I mean a day in which you restore your soul. Perhaps this conjures up images of stern pioneers observing the Sabbath by attending church and then reading Scripture or religious material all day long and avoiding any noise or play. If we carry those images, we might think of the Sabbath as a day of restrictions and prohibitions. I believe, rather, that keeping the Sabbath is about privileges and freedom. It is a day when we can leave our work behind and enter into the "being" phase of life rather than concentrating on the "doing." It is not just a day to stop working; it is a day to stop thinking about work as well. We recall well the Bible story about God creating the world in six days and resting on the seventh. Scripture views rest as a divine activity, not a sign of laziness or weakness but rather one of wisdom and holiness.

Picture a day in which you allow yourself to rejoice in sensual and emotional pleasures—a day of wonderful food, good company, the quiet pleasures of a walk, a good book, gorgeous flowers in your garden, or even a little romance. Treat yourself royally! Set the table with your favorite dishes, put a vase of flowers on the table, light a candle, take time to pray and reflect.

I often wonder how our lives would change if one day each week we quit taking phone calls, racing around town in our cars doing errands, and flipping television channels. I try to imagine what it would feel like to stop spending money on shopping excursions and looking to the outside world for entertainment and distraction. I believe our lives would change significantly if for one day a week we left behind the world of materialism, technology, and busyness and entered into a world of nature, beauty, reflection, and spiritual attentiveness. Such true rest would give us a completely different perspective on life's difficulties. It would allow us to put the events and pressures of our lives into perspective, reflect as we turn things over to our Creator to manage, express gratitude for all we are and have, heal, and face whatever lies ahead with a renewed sense of self and of calm.

We cannot experience such a Sabbath without a little forethought. Unless we make a conscious commitment and do a little planning, we will likely discover that we quickly skip into leftover things on our to-do list, such as shopping, cleaning, errands, and working on the materials in our briefcases. We might take a lesson from our Jewish brothers and sisters, who take a day to prepare for Sabbath. Jews who observe the Sabbath get their work done before Friday sundown. Then all work stops, a candle is lit, and a glass of wine is placed on the table as the Sabbath is begun with simple prayers.

I recommend that you find some way to ritualize the beginning of your Sabbath rest. Perhaps start it with a song, a few scripture verses, and some moments of complete silence as you center yourself and get in touch with your body and soul again. Then light a candle. Likewise, ritualize the end of your Sabbath. At a concluding evening meal, offer prayers of thanksgiving for the Sabbath rest and the gift of work to which you will return. Or sing a special song. An old Jewish custom is to pass around a box of sweet smelling spices as a reminder of the fragrance of Sabbath that needs to permeate the entire week ahead. A similar act for Christians could be accompanied by a prayer of gratitude for the Spirit of the risen Christ who empowers us with purpose and hope, and for the guidance of the Spirit as we care for the earth and its people during the week ahead.

Clergy and perhaps other church staff members will likely find that Sunday cannot be their Sabbath. Those who study the pressures and complexities of clergy roles, as I have, find that clergy put in the equivalent of a ten-hour day between the hours of eight and noon on Sunday. After two worship services and teaching an adult class when I was a parish pastor, I was so tired I had to spend Sunday afternoons sleeping! Clergy usually have to do the things other members take care of on Saturdays—mow the lawn, do the laundry, get a haircut, and go grocery shopping. I suggest that clergy, therefore, negotiate with their congregations to have two days off per week, one for life-maintenance tasks and one for Sabbath. If clergy really did observe a day of Sabbath, I am confident that I would no longer find that 40 percent of clergy in my workshops would score exceedingly high on the Burnout Rating Scale.[6]

We live in a culture that values doing rather than being. But when all of life is consumed by doing, something vital is lost. Other aspects of our life begin to suffer—our health, relationships, spirituality, emotional well-being, and even our work. People who do not take off time just to be typically find that they have less energy and creativity to bring to their paid work. Much of the current literature on leadership stresses the quality of authenticity. Remaining an authentic, integrated human being does not happen by accident. It requires time simply to be and to gain some distance and perspective on our life. Practicing the ritual of Sabbath rest is one of the very best ways of ritualizing the value of our being.

Ritualizing Life Transitions

Ritualizing the many transitions in life is like putting markers along the way, so we can look back at them. It is an opportunity to point to the God who creates, redeems, and sustains us throughout life. The church has marked some of these transitions for hundreds of years. Faith communities celebrate birth with baptism, our transition to adulthood with confirmation, our commitments of intimacy in marriage, and our death with a funeral and burial rituals. It has been the task of the church to make the word of God relevant in every age. As we enter a new millennium, the church falls short in its mission if it only continues to ritualize these traditional turning points in the life of members. As is discussed in this book's introduction, people today experience many more transitions than in the past. We are now experiencing a rapidity and breadth of change never experienced before. Most of us move through multiple transition processes simultaneously and wonder why we feel tired, discouraged, and broken. We wonder where to turn for assistance to deal with external changes and the struggle of internal transitions. The church has not provided nearly the degree and depth of assistance that I believe it is now called to offer.

The transformation of human life is always a mysterious process and eludes our attempts to explain why and how the transformation comes about. We confess that we believe, in the midst of all transitions, that the Spirit is active among us and calls us to partnership in the work of making lives full of meaning, wholeness, and faith. As individuals in families, friendships, congregations, and neighborhoods, we are called by God to be present to others in caring ways as they journey through endings, the haze of the neutral zones, and toward new beginnings. We can share our stories, care, and spiritual resources. On a congregational level, we can organize ministries in such a way that as the local expression of the body of Christ, we assist people to move toward spiritual transformation by helping them to ritualize these transitional journeys. Let us turn to several specific illustrations of rituals that acknowledge the stages of such transitions in the lives of individuals, families, and friendship groups.

A Child Entering School

Important rituals in families sometimes acknowledge that a specific transition is primarily an ending for some members of the family and constitutes primarily a new beginning for others. For example, when a small child begins to attend school, whether that is preschool, kindergarten, or first grade, an exciting new adventure is beginning for the child, but for the first time, the child's parents will not have the child at home for a significant portion of each weekday. The child will be going out into the wider world and building significant relationships beyond the family. As in all transitions, something is lost and something else is gained. A child who has been eager to go to school will primarily experience the new beginning, and the parent of that child might feel pangs of loss. Engaging in creative ritual at such a time helps this family sum up the entirety of the experience in symbolic form. Here is an illustration of what such a ritual might be like.

The child and parent or parents could together create something that would remind one another of their continued love and support while they are separated for this period of time each day. For example, the parent might make a small pin for the child to wear that symbolizes the presence of the parent. Or a heart-shaped locket containing a picture of the whole family could be hung around the child's neck. The child might make a cutout of a doll and tape it to a kitchen chair, symbolizing her ongoing presence with the mother. At dinner the evening before or at breakfast on the first day of school, the family could hold hands to ask a blessing for the occasion. The child might choose the menu for this meal. Other children in the family could make drawings or provide a picture that illustrates their hopes for the new student. For example, a picture of two young children holding hands might symbolize the child's ability to make friends easily.

Adolescent Mile Markers

In our culture, puberty and adolescence can be awkward and even painful for both parents and young people. Wishing to avoid any discomfort or embarrassment, families might be inclined to avoid ritualizing these transition experiences. Families could discover, however, that taking the risk to develop appropriate rituals marking the various transitions involved in puberty and adolescence will actually make these transitions easier for everyone involved.

One family raising daughters planned three special rituals for each of them. The first was held as each girl approached puberty. The women in the family—grandmothers, aunts, cousins, and the godmothers—joined the daughters and their mother for the celebration. Each woman was invited to bring a story of someone or something that was helpful to her in her own adolescence. She was also asked to bring a token of her blessing for the daughter in whose honor the ritual celebration was being held. The tokens provided a way for the girl to remember the blessings offered her. In one celebration, as each woman offered her blessing of the girl, the one giving the blessing dropped a flower petal into a bowl of water. All of this was incorporated into a prayer service, which is included in appendix D on page 135. After the stories and tokens had been shared, participants each mentioned a way that the young girl had been a blessing to them and then toasted her with raspberry tea. The service concluded with a final sending forth of the daughter. Though the ritual celebrations were somewhat similar for the two girls, their mother built some differences into the rituals based on what she saw as the archetype for each daughter—for one, movement from chaos to order, and for the other, movement from fear to courage.

Upon conclusion of the ritual, the girl's father arrived at the front door with roses and asked, "Is there a young woman here?" The women of the family responded, "Yes, here she is!" and presented the daughter to the father. Then other male relatives arrived and all shared in a dinner whose menu was chosen by the daughter.

The second milemarker of adolescence, menstruation, was celebrated by this family with a special dinner. No particular conversation about menstruation occurred at the dinner, yet the meal celebrated all that was now happening in the young woman's life. The mother shared a poem acknowledging that her daughter was now also her sister through a shared womanhood.

The third stage of adolescent ritual will occur when each daughter graduates from high school. Although that ritual has not yet been designed, it will focus on helping the daughter reflect on how far she has come in her journey and the ways in which she has been a blessing to the family and those around them. The ritual will conclude with blessings for the next stage of the young women's journeys.[7]

In a culture in which we have few healthy rituals for acknowledging that our sons and daughters are moving from childhood to adulthood, such rituals as these can be very important celebrations. Appropriate parallel rituals could be developed for sons in a family.

Simple rituals might also be designed for other key events in an adolescent's life. For example, receiving a driver's license is generally considered significant. To celebrate this event through ritual, family and friends gather and form a prayer circle. The teenager brings her new driver's license as well as a symbol of her childhood such as a children's book, doll, or other toy. Group members place their hands on the license to bless it and pray that God will help the young person to be responsible with her new privilege and keep her safe. She, in turn covenants to drive carefully in order to protect her own life and that of others and announces the contribution of the childhood symbol to a child in need, thus recognizing that she is giving up the innocence of childhood and will be relying less on her parents.

Rituals for the Waiting Zone

Among the most difficult times to ritualize are the neutral zones— times of waiting and confusion. Such times often lead to flailing about for quick solutions or immobilizing depression and despair. Rituals can help us through this challenging stage of the transition process, which is fertile soil for transformation.

•   *Waiting in abstinence*: Rituals can help young people affirm the anxious waiting period between the onset of puberty and the time when they engage in responsible sex within a committed relationship of marriage. It is essential that teens and young adults themselves be involved in the design of such rituals and the choice to participate in them or not. Such rituals might occur within a congregation itself or within families or groups of friends. Likely such rituals would include both a written covenant and a verbal declaration surrounded by prayer, perhaps the use of a slogan or motto, and conversation about why such important choices are being made.

•   *Preparing for next steps after high school*: An anxious time occurs for teenagers and young adults as they try to decide what they will do after high school—attend college or technical school, take a full-time job, enter the armed services, and so forth. This can be an especially difficult time for young people if most of their friends have already determined what their future steps will be. But such a transitional time also holds the promise of important lessons in patience, self-confidence, and remaining centered in the midst of uncertainty. Try regular acknowledgment of this time of waiting during prayer at family meals or family meetings. Offer petitions of patience, anticipation, expectancy, and surrender to doors that might open. Invite members of the family to share stories about their own times of waiting, whether as children or as adults. Reflect together on the difference between experiences approached with patient waiting for what might come rather than compulsive action to seek a quick fix for one's anxiety. Light a candle of expectancy at each evening meal. Read the Magnificat, the song of Mary as she willingly waits to be a servant of God in whatever uncertain future transpires for her, and the story of Simeon and Anna, who waited many years to witness the birth of the one who was to be a "light for revelation to the Gentiles and for glory to your people Israel" (Luke 2:32). These two went to the temple each day, waiting to see how God was going to deliver his people.

Rituals during Illness

A middle-aged professional woman, by her own admission a somewhat impatient person, had a long-dreamed-of sabbatical interrupted by illness. Days of uncertainty stretched into weeks as she returned to her home, underwent numerous medical tests, and waited for results, a diagnosis, and treatment. In order to deal with her feelings of anger, sadness, discouragement, and fear, she gradually designed a series of daily rituals.

First, she invited and welcomed the prayer support of family, friends, and colleagues and regularly updated many of them by E-mail about her progress. Although she sometimes felt such updates might be seen as self-pity, she nevertheless continued to write in an effort to remain connected with others and allow them to support her during a difficult time. A regular journaler, she increased attention to her gratitude list, wrote letters to God, and added affirmations and images of healing to her journal pages. During times of reflection, she repeatedly asked herself, "Where did I experience God today?" and "What am I learning from this period of disappointment, uncertainty, weakness, and discouragement?"

As she found herself increasingly agitated from lack of sleep, the frustrations of dealing with medical systems, and waiting for more information about her illness, she sought to regain a sense of calm and order by returning to an abbreviated version of her familiar daily schedule of work, exercise, and conversation with friends. During intimidating medical procedures, she often imagined God standing right beside her, massaging her shoulders, and speaking softly with encouraging words and promises of ongoing presence and protection. At such times she regularly identified other people who were in crisis or pain and offered her experiences as a prayer for their comfort and healing.

As the weeks stretched on without a clear diagnosis, she sometimes was surprised to find that she was becoming more centered and
that she felt surrounded by the prayers of family, friends, and colleagues.
As she settled into prayer and journaling in the evening—the time of
day she had come to dread because of her difficulty in sleeping—she
lit one of the light green votive candles she had chosen as symbols of
hope and promise of healing. Even before she knew the final results of
the medical tests or the suggested course of treatment, she began to
imagine how she would use her learnings in her ministry of writing
and education. What she had heretofore known mostly through her
intellect about the anxiety and sense of loss associated with illness, she
now understood from personal experience. Having experienced this
form of vulnerability, she knew that she would never be quite the same
person again.

Ritual Acknowledging Personal Transformation

Sometimes individual rituals can be designed to clearly symbolize a
major transformation. Designing such rituals will be intensely personal
and call forth our unique creativity. Let me share one from my own life
that had great meaning for me.

Several years ago, while on a spiritual retreat in a remote setting in
the desert hills of Arizona, I concluded that I no longer wanted to live
with a frightened, low self-image of myself. I wished for more joy,
celebration, and laughter. I found myself tired of allowing fear to domi-
nate my life as much as it had. One afternoon, I took a long hike with
my daypack into a wooded area on top of a butte. There I searched for
a certain kind of brush whose lower branches formed an opening I
could crawl through. When I finally found what I was looking for, I
placed my daypack on the opposite side of the bushes and lay down
on the ground to contemplate what I was undertaking. I wanted to
experience a rebirth. I knew that meant I had to leave my old self behind and take on a new self. As I lay there, I allowed myself to grieve
the self that I was choosing to give up. In some ways, it had served me
well through many years, yet I knew it had outlived its purpose. I found
myself shedding tears for what was to be left behind, but I knew part of
me needed to die before something new could be born in me. And so I
grieved that death.

After about 45 minutes of such reflective grieving, I felt ready for a new birth. I took off my old clothes and, with some difficulty, crawled through the brush to the other side and changed into a new set of clothes from my daypack. Then I found a flat stone nearby and began to dance on it. I felt wonderful as I celebrated my new self. This ritual symbolized for me the dying to an old self and transformation into a new life. Other people will find other ways that might better express such a transformation in their own lives.

Other Transition Rituals for Individuals and Families

Of course, there are many other opportunities for ritualizing transitions in our individual and family lives. Below are several descriptions of such rituals.

•   *Ritual acknowledging aging parent*: Some family situations might involve a painful ending. This happened in my family around our Christmas traditions. All members of my family of origin live in Canada—my two younger sisters in western Canada and my two older brothers in eastern Canada. Because the great distances made it difficult for us to get together over Christmas, my mother, who lived in Saskatchewan, alternated between the two sets of families every other Christmas. My wife, Carole, and I typically spent Christmas with the eastern siblings and thus saw my mother at Christmas every second year. On the day after Christmas, which is Boxing Day in Canada, nearly 25 members of our family always rented a curling or skating rink to celebrate, because neither of my brothers' homes would hold us all. There, after four generations of us enjoyed curling or skating, we went to the clubhouse to share a simple meal, open gifts, and move into a big circle to sing Christmas carols. Our last carol was always "Silent Night."

The year my mother turned ninety, she had announced to us that this would be her last Christmas in Ontario, because she felt she was getting too old to travel. It seemed important to recognize such a significant ending, so as we planned this last Christmas gathering with our mother, I asked Mother whether she would be comfortable with us cradling her during the singing of the last carol. She agreed, and so

with everyone on their feet, four pairs of adults stood around Mother
and asked her to receive this ritual as an expression of the ongoing
support she would receive from us. As she leaned back, we picked her
up and gently began to rock her back and forth while we sang all three
verses of "Silent Night." The remaining adults and children in the room
gathered close and placed their hands on those doing the rocking. Near
the end of the carol, we slowly lowered my mother to the floor and
knelt around to lay hands on her and offer prayers acknowledging that
my mother faced an uncertain future, one different from what she or
we had known. At the conclusion of these individual prayers, we prayed
the Lord's Prayer together and helped Mother to her feet. Then individuals came forward, embraced her, and wished her well.

This was an especially moving expression of unity as well as one
of loss for our family. In fact, that was the last time many of my nieces
and nephews and their children got to be with their grandmother. It
was for all of us our last Christmas with her.

• *Acknowledgment that death is near*: Living during a time of easy
access to immense medical resources and in a death-avoiding culture,
we can easily get caught in the fight to stay alive at all costs, to endure
unending use of technology and painful efforts to sustain our life when
it is clear such an effort only postpones the inevitable. Clearly, different people and families make different decisions about how long to
fight for life and when to accept that the end of life is near. Rituals at
some point, however, will assist both the dying person and their loved
ones to reach meaningful closure. A wide variety of rituals can help us
in such situations. The dying person might wish to have an opportunity to resolve differences and make peace with those with whom he
has experienced conflict; see and bless specific friends, colleagues,
and family members; or review his journey and relationships with others through story telling, picture sharing, or journaling.

Relationships with family and friends might be celebrated ritually
by gathering for conversation, sharing a glass of wine, and offering a
prayer of thanksgiving. The dying person might bless each of those
who has come and express thanks for the ways each person has been a
blessing in his life. In return, those present could each thank and bless
the dying person for the place he had in their lives. As family and
friends gather around the dying person—holding hands or laying hands

on him— they can share in prayer and sing favorite hymns or other special music to him as an expression of their love and good-byes.

• *Death of a family member*: The wife and five grown children of a man stood at his bedside in a hospice as he neared death from a rapidly advancing cancer. As he died, they sprinkled golden angel confetti in his hair and wrapped him in a batik shawl with symbols of the universe on it that his daughter had recently purchased. The family stayed with their husband and father for several hours after his death. In the days of preparation for the funeral, his wife wore the shawl. Several grand-children sprinkled golden angels throughout the house and down the front steps. They drew chalk drawings of angels, stars, and god's eyes on the sidewalk and made a large poster of their grandfather and grand-mother with the words "We love you, Grandpa" printed on it. The obituary in the newspaper read: "In the presence of his wife and five children, he returned to the loving embrace of his Creator."[8]

• *Moving on after a loss*: These rituals might be used in a variety of situations, including loss of health, job, or other significant losses. They acknowledge all three stages of a transition. The first phase recognizes the setback. Invite friends and family to join you for the ritual, explain-ing what loss has taken place and the impact it is having on you. Ask that people consider bringing an object or symbol that might help you deal with the loss. As part of the ritual, people may express their sup-port and concern by explaining the story of their gift. After sharing food and drink together, invite those present to offer an expression of connection and support such as joining in a group hug, offering a prayer while holding hands in a circle, or singing a blessing while extending their hands over you in a gesture of blessing, or another appropriate act of love and caring.

During the anxious, waiting time while you search for a job, await the result of medical tests, or enter into treatment for an illness, keep your family and friends informed about your experiences and feel-ings. There are many ways to do this. Write a short reflection every few days, and mail it to those who are sharing your journey, or send an E-mail message regularly updating them. Encourage people to be in touch with you and offer you their support.

Once the situation begins to resolve itself or a breakthrough oc-curs (finding a job, healing from physical illness or coming to terms with it), plan a celebration of new beginning. The character of the actual celebration would depend on the specific loss that was experienced and the nature of the new beginning. But undoubtedly it would include sharing food and drink, perhaps singing and dancing, prayer, sharing appropriate symbols of the new beginning and the love and support you have received during the transition, and a group blessing for the new stage of your journey.

•   *Leaving on a long trip*: When a family member leaves on an extended trip, the entire family might get together for a meal. A large, thick candle is lit. The family promises to keep a lit candle on the dinner table for as long as the individual is away, thereby acknowledging the symbolic presence of that person. The family could also give the traveler a small candle to light each evening. Both the traveler and the family members remaining at home might covenant to light their candle and pray for one other each day.

•   *Welcoming a new family pet*: Family pets tend to work their way into the hearts and lives of most people in a household. A ritual recognizing this fact is often a great way to begin this new relationship. Family members gather around the pet and, if the pet has not already been named, explore possible names. After discussion, consensus might be reached on a name or, alternatively, the youngest member of the family might name the pet. A food might be shared that could be enjoyed by both the pet and the people in the family. After sharing the morsels of food, the members of the family gather in a circle, lift up the pet, stroke it, and call it by its new name.

•   *Going on a spiritual pilgrimage*: Although traditional pilgrimages have fallen into disuse, we have the opportunity to design unique spiritual pilgrimages for ourselves. You might make your pilgrimage by traveling on foot to a place near home, visiting a developing nation, going on sabbatical or retreat, or in some other way breaking out of your familiar routine. Such experiences are rich with opportunities to view ourselves and our world in a new way. You will create your own unique way of ritualizing such experiences.

A middle-aged female colleague of mine celebrated her fiftieth birthday with a six-week backpacking trip—a third of which she did solo with her dog. This was a conscious reframing of her lifelong dream to do an even more extensive hike along one of the country's transcontinental trails. She announced her commitment to this physical and spiritual journey and the reframing of her life dream by mailing a personal letter to friends and colleagues several months in advance of her trip. In her letter, she asked for their prayers, support, and possible participation. Then she set out to pick up special stones both at a significant trail juncture and from the end of the trail she would hike months later. She added the stones to a packet of tokens that symbolized special people in her life: a decade of her mother's rosary, a cedar leaf from her father's grave, a camping list once shared with her former husband and hiking partner, and moss from the point where her north woods cabin stood. As time for her trek drew near, she invited her mother to help her organize and pack food and supplies for the trip. The night before her departure, she shared a special meal with a close friend who gave her the children's book *The Little Engine That Could*.[9]

Tucked inside her backpack as she began her walk were the two stones and other symbols as well as a journal and tape recorder, so she could keep track of her experiences, reflections, and feelings during her journey. Midway through her journey, as she crossed the trail juncture near her cabin, she returned the first stone from her symbol packet to the trail, and then several family members and friends met her for a special meal. Two weeks later, as she and a close friend neared the end of the trek, they used the tape recorder she carried and interviewed one another about their self-discoveries. And when she took the final step of her journey, she reached down and returned the second stone from her symbol packet to the place where she had first picked it up several months earlier when she had committed to the journey. After returning to her urban home, all who had been involved in sharing her physical and spiritual pilgrimage gathered for a party to share pictures and stories as well as food and drink. An unintended outcome of that final celebration was the emergence of an informal intergenerational prayer chain that linked the concerns of these women over the years that followed.[10]

Further Opportunities for Ritualizing

We experience both major and minor transitions. Each of these changes has the potential for breaking open new meaning and depth in our lives. Such possibilities are enhanced when we intentionally create ways of ritualizing these transitions. Below is a list of many such opportunities.

- Miscarriage (see ritual in appendix A, page 127)
- Divorce
- Learning one is pregnant
- Adopting a child
- Naming a child
- A child's first words and first steps
- Beginning and ending grades or stages of school
- Learning a new skill such as riding a bicycle or using a computer
- First communion, confirmation
- Deciding to marry
- Leaving a familiar home, apartment, or community
- Moving into a new home or apartment
- Remarrying and blending families
- Retiring from a job and career
- Moving into an assisted living facility or nursing home
- Aging
- Emptying the nest
- Beginning joint custody of children
- Waiting to have a child
- Giving up a driver's license due to age or illness
- Adults beginning or completing an educational program or degree
- Adults beginning a new renewal effort such as entering spiritual direction, a Twelve Step program, becoming part of a small faith sharing group, or joining a church
- Entering or completing treatment or therapy
- Leaving for or returning from an extended vacation or sabbatical
- Celebrating a special life achievement
- Waiting for the results of major medical tests
- Facing a major illness and loss of health

- Recovery from an illness
- Experiencing individual or family joy or surprise
- Taking a family member off life support systems

Reflection Exercises

1. Recall any occasions on which you have created a new daily ritual for yourself. Reflect on the meaning it brought to your life.

2. Design a ritual for a transition you are currently experiencing or have recently experienced.

3. With family members or friends, work together to plan and then carry out a ritual celebration for a transitional situation.

4. Discuss this chapter with a group in your congregation. Share stories of your experiences with transitional rituals as individuals or with family and friends. Discuss your favorite examples in this chapter.

CHAPTER 4

Ritualizing in the Congregation

You might wonder why we need to bother with transitional rituals within the congregation itself. After all, in our Sunday worship services we celebrate the transitions in the liturgical year, and as congregations, we pay considerable attention to rituals for baptism, confirmation, marriage, and burial. Many other rituals that acknowledge changes in people's personal lives can be celebrated in the home or with neighborhood friends. It might seem that we already have enough rituals. Yet the church needs continually to evaluate how even its traditional rituals related to word and sacrament can be kept fresh and meaningful in the lives of members. And many individual transitions—such as adopting children, having a miscarriage, finding one's calling in life, or retiring—are not usually marked by ritual but might be made more a part of ourselves by both home-based and congregation-based ritualizing.

In addition, many congregational leaders are not alert for the stages of endings, the neutral waiting times, and new beginnings that occur throughout congregational life—starting and concluding programs and campaigns, doing strategic planning, handling conflict, changing leaders. Because we often discount the emotional content of these communal, organizational transitions, we miss the opportunity to bring ritual to bear on them. We lose the chance to mine these transitions for communal meaning and transformation.

Attentiveness to congregational transitions as well as those of a personal and family nature on the one hand, and those in the societal arena on the other, can help members of the church better integrate all the experiences of change and transition that affect them. Insight, healing, and new growth in one context can assist us in finding transformation in other contexts as well. As William Bridges wrote, "[S]ome of the feelings you experience today have nothing to do with the present ending but come, instead, from old associations. What you bring with you to any transitional situation is a style that you have developed for dealing with endings."[1] Because all transitions begin with some kind of an ending, it is true that the styles we developed for dealing with earlier transitions affect our future approaches to transition. The church can enrich both its own health as an institution as well as the individual and communal lives of its members by being alert to all transition processes within its own life and ministry and employing ritual as one way of capturing these possibilities for transformation.

Rituals for Individual and Family Changes

First, we will explore transitions that might be ritualized in the home but that would have additional meaning and possibilities for growth if also acknowledged within faith communities themselves. Some transitions, such as confirmation and a child's baptism or dedication, which are already major celebrations in the church, might simply need updated and enriched ritual processes and symbols. Others, such as children going to school, moving from one's home to a condo or apartment, or becoming homebound, might provide new opportunities for the church to minister with members.

Rituals for Confirmation

Sociologists, psychologists, and anthropologists agree that in the West we are largely bereft of meaningful rituals that mark the passage of boys and girls into adulthood. In chapter 3 we explored some possible home rituals related to these passages. Here I would like to suggest rituals that could take place in the congregation itself to highlight this important transition in the lives of our teenagers today.

I sometimes wince when I recall how I tried as a parish pastor to teach young people who were preparing for confirmation. I thought it was my responsibility to give them as much information about Christianity as they could possibly absorb. Today my confirmation classes would be much more basic. I would spend a great deal of time on prayer. I would inquire about their individual experiences of prayer, what they had been taught about it, how they had experienced family prayer, and the role prayer has had for them as adolescents. I would encourage them to covenant to spend at least ten minutes each day in prayer. Each confirmation preparation session would involve some way for them to talk about what they had experienced in their daily ten minutes of prayer, what they found easy or comforting, what was difficult or disconcerting.

As part of the journey toward confirmation I would ask each teen to select an adult as his or her confirmation mentor or sponsor. Each mentor would be encouraged to meet with the confirmand several times during the preparation process to discuss becoming an adult Christian, share and talk about prayer, review the service project the teen has chosen, and share talk about how each perceives the call to ministry in daily life. The leaders of the mentoring program might provide several brief discussion guides for the pairs to help them talk about topics such as the role faith plays when making decisions, and so forth.

As the confirmation preparation period begins, each young person, his or her parents, and the chosen mentor would be invited to an elegant candle-lit meal prepared by members of the church. The meal would conclude with a ritual of commitment marking this passage, the beginning of the formal mentoring relationships that would continue throughout the several-month preparation process for confirmation.

Two or three times during the following months, the confirmands would come before the congregation to share their insights and commitments. Once, for example, each person might make a short statement about discoveries in the life of faith and prayer. Another time, the confirmands could announce the service project that they had chosen. Finally, they would affirm their commitment to participate in the final confirmation ritual itself. It is important that this choice is the young person's and not simply engaged in because of social convention or parental pressure. On the occasion of their confirmation, they would be joined by their mentors and be asked to give a very brief statement about their commitment to the spiritual journey.

Either before or after the confirmation ceremony, the group of young people would be responsible for planning and providing leadership for a Sunday worship service—including doing the readings, choosing music, collaborating on the preaching on a given theme, and perhaps, depending on the nature of the theme, they could gather or design resources they might distribute to the adults in the congregation. If there are only a few confirmands in the congregation, other members might be in charge of adult education and the coffee hour on that Sunday, but adult members of the congregation will likely be delighted by the creativity and fresh perspectives and commitments these young people offer and find them good teachers.

Other Rituals for Individuals

•   *Baptism or child dedication*: When a couple comes to inquire about having their child baptized or dedicated, this is an excellent opportunity to talk with the parents about engaging in family patterns that will help ensure their child is rooted in the Christian faith. Whether the pastor, designated staff member, or trained lay minister leads the preparation for this special event, they can make the case that the way Christianity is lived in the home has a larger effect on the child than what the child is taught in the congregation itself. Make suggestions for engaging in prayer as a family, and offer the parents appropriate print resources.[2] Share the practice of making the sign of the cross on the forehead of the child each night when putting the child to bed. If several couples are involved in a baptismal/dedication preparation class, have them work together to brainstorm rituals they might use with their children. The parents will be more receptive to ritual practices they themselves have created.

•   *Ritual for a miscarriage*: When Jean and Tim married, they invited others to witness and bless their marriage and shared a goal they had for their relationship—to be light for one another and for others. In their early 40s, Jean and Tim suffered the loss of a second pregnancy, which was particularly difficult, given their ages. Again, they turned to ritual. They gathered objects that told part of their story—the goblet and plate made for the eucharistic celebration of their marriage, a sculpture of children encircling a votive candle, a baptismal cross inscribed with the words "Let Your Light Shine," and a small woven basket with a lid, a place of rest for the spirit of their unborn child. The couple, a pastor, and a family representative gathered together to share prayer, tears, and a simple story.[3]

• *Ritual for an adoption*: Some months later, the symbol of light was present again when Jean and Tim adopted three sisters from Siccum, India. They all went to their church and read again the readings from the couple's wedding. Jean and Tim then made their commitment to each of their new adopted daughters. Each girl was given a gold necklace, the star of India on a chain, each of the five points of the star representing a member of their family and reminding them that a star shines brightly in the darkness. The girl's mother has a star necklace, too, and their father wears a star lapel pin. Again, the light shines in the darkness![4]

• *Ritual for a divorce*: Many members of the church who experience the pain of divorce would welcome some sort of ritualizing of this ending of an important chapter and relationship in their lives. However, because the circumstances of divorce are individual, these rituals are likely to include only family or close friends or perhaps only the divorced person. It is important that anyone suggesting such ritualizing or providing resources for the divorced be sensitive to the considerable shame often experienced by those who divorce as well as the state of the relationship between former spouses, which will depend on the nature of the divorce. It is essential that all decisions about the ritual be made by the divorced person. To force a ritual on a person would be to victimize someone who might already feel like a victim.

One woman, divorced at age 41, for example, waited several years before she felt ready to create a personal ritual recognizing the loss of her marriage. She chose to return alone to the church where she had been married. She began by walking to the very spot in the sanctuary where she had once taken her vows and there, in an empty church, acknowledged in a whisper that the marriage she had so valued was over. Then taking a seat nearby, she quietly remembered the many good times in her relationship with her husband and all the many ways she had grown. She thanked God and her spouse for those times. She recalled the prayers that had been said the day of the wedding, the words of the hymns that were sung, and the sermon preached on that day. Next she reflected on the painful times in the latter days of the marriage and gradually let them go. Then once again she walked out down the aisle, this time as a single person. In the gathering space of the church, she stopped and stood quietly in the very spot

she remembered waiting with her spouse, her parents, and his to receive greetings from those attending the marriage ceremony. Finally,
she left the church alone. Although others might have chosen to create
a public ritual, for her the ritual was more meaningful done in private.
But she wanted to do her ritualizing in the sanctuary of the church
building.

Other Rituals for Groups

•   *Children beginning school*: Children entering kindergarten or first
grade and their parents are invited to the front of the nave. Two litanies
could be written—one for the parents and the other for the children.
The first would be read responsively between the pastor and the parents and focus on the parents' willingness to relinquish some of their
oversight of the child to other adults in the community. It would address both the loss and sense of new beginning in this transition. The
parents then return to their pews as a sign that they are ready to let go,
to some degree, of their children.

    The children's litany could be more informal. The children might
gather around the worship leader and talk about what they will miss
most about not being at home all day. The conversation would then
shift to what excites them about beginning school. Each child might
bring a toy they are willing to give up as they take on the new role of
student. These toys could then be donated to an agency that serves
children in need. Finally, the congregation might sing a blessing to
these children. "Go With Us, Lord," sung to the tune Tallis Canon,
might be appropriate.[5]

•   *First communion*: Children with their families, including godpar-
ents, come forward one family at a time to receive communion. The
children's sermon focuses on Jesus' promise that he will be with us
each time we eat bread and drink wine together in this fashion. The
children who are to receive communion are encouraged to be open to
sensing the presence of Jesus as they receive the communion elements.
Other children who are not yet prepared for receiving the eucharist are
reminded that they will be soon able to participate with their parents in
preparing for this sacrament. Adults in the congregation are encouraged to greet the first communicants on this Sunday, and families are

urged to have celebrations for friends and family in their homes following the service.

• *High school or college graduation*: During a regular weekend worship service, high school and college graduates are invited to come forward and each briefly share what is coming next in their lives. They might be asked to name something for which they are especially grateful in their education or a special time, teacher, or mentor who was important to them in their educational process. Congregational prayers are then offered in support of the young people entering the next stage of their lives.

• *Celebration of vocation and ministry in daily life*: In today's church, we are again rightfully emphasizing that God calls all people and reemphasizing the ministry of the laity in daily life. Congregations make a powerful statement about this universal calling when they ritualize it in some way. Once a year, for example, a congregation might hold a commissioning service during which all members of the church are commissioned into a shared ministry. In addition, ordination or commissioning rituals might be held for individuals or groups of people who feel called by God to serve as teachers, physicians, firefighters, farmers, engineers, or community volunteers. The planners of the ritual can consult their denomination's book of special services and follow the ritual for ordinations. Sermons might be build around scripture readings on calling such as Micah 6:8; 1 Samuel 3:1-18; Exodus 3:11; 4:1, 10, 13; Jeremiah 1:6; and Luke 1:26-38. Hymns could include "Called as Partners in Christ's Service," "Here I Am, Lord," "We Are Called,"[6] or other related hymns.

Such a service could be structured in numerous ways. Representatives of various professions could be part of an offertory procession and each bring forward a symbol of that profession. A plumber might bring a wrench; a doctor or nurse, a stethoscope; a farmer, a bag of seed; a student, a book; a secretary, pages of computer printouts; a parent, children's storybooks and toys; and so forth.

A large cake could be decorated with the symbols of various walks of life and served at a party following the worship service. At the party, an information booth could make available information on career development, and a gifts assessment, and a display of books on vocation, gifts discovery, and ministry in daily life.[7]

•   *Beginning retirement:* When it becomes known that a member of the congregation is planning to retire, someone trained to help people discern their gifts and calling might talk with the person, not to engage the retiree in some specific new ministry of the congregation but to reflect with the person on his years of work and the meaning they held for him and to explore what he is looking forward to and feeling called toward in this new chapter in his life. (My personal observation is that people who do well in retirement are those who feel called to do something or be someone new.)

Once a year, all those who have retired during the calendar year or who will soon retire are asked to come forward during the worship service and to bring a symbol of something that represents their former job or role in life. These symbols can be placed in front of the altar, on the communion rail, or handed to the pastor or members of the ministry in daily life committee, if the congregation has such a ministry. The retirees might offer a brief reflection about their years of employment and what they sense God might be calling them to in the next stage of life. The worship leader would then offer a prayer of thanksgiving and concern for the transition these people are entering. The ritual would conclude with people kneeling at the communion rail and receiving a commissioning to their next vocation with the laying on of hands and offering of prayers, followed by a benediction. A formal reception or a more informal pot luck meal following the service would allow the other members of the congregation to talk individually with retirees, offer support, and indicate ongoing interest in their vocations.

•   *Ritual for those giving up their house*: Today there is a less age-related distinction among those who choose to leave single-family dwellings for townhouse, condominium, or apartment living. Younger people are doing it all the time. This particular transition, however, is often more marked among senior adults because of the reason for the move: they find it more difficult to keep up their own homes. A simple ritual might acknowledge that this transition constitutes both an ending and a new beginning. The ritual might be conducted as a congregational event or in small groups such as women's circles, men's groups, couple's groups, retirement groups, and so forth. Key to this ritual is having participants bring symbols of what they are giving up as well as their hopes for the good things they believe lie ahead of them in this new living arrangement.

If only a few people are ritualizing this transition, each person should be encouraged to say a few words about their decision, their grief, and their hope. Prayers or a litany should affirm the joys of the years in their own homes as well as the possibilities for new freedom in the coming months and years.

•   *Ritual for those about to be homebound*: Family, friends, and neighbors will want to be part of this ritual to demonstrate the caring circle of people for each older or physically challenged or ill person. If possible, family members or friends could escort the person in transition to be presented to the congregation. The ritual honors in a special way the gift of courage that is required to remain positive about life's possibilities. The immediate circle of family and friends as well as the larger congregation pledge themselves to remain in touch with the homebound, even when this person can no longer attend church services or functions. If trained lay ministers such as BeFrienders or Stephen Ministers, in addition to members and friends, are part of the ongoing ministry to the homebound, these lay ministers should participate in the service and be designated as official visitors on behalf of the congregation and its ministry. Clergy, lay leaders, family, and lay ministers would all lay hands on those entering the homebound stage of life, committing to pray for, visit, and uphold the homebound member as part of that faith and neighborhood community.

Transitions in the Congregation's Ministry

Congregations are continually undergoing transitions in their organizational, programmatic, and leadership dimensions. Many of these transitions pass almost unrecognized by most members. Other transitions are more visible but rarely ritualized. Because we so seldom have named the stages of transition through which our congregations are passing, we often are puzzled and frustrated by the reactions of those around us and might be quick to discount their feelings or to assign dishonorable motives to them. Congregational transitions are opportunities for spiritual growth, deepening community, and communal transformation. Ritualizing them in appropriate and creative ways helps our congregations tap into these possibilities.

Beginning a Strategic Planning Effort

One of the most significant undertakings of any congregation is the initiation of a strategic planning or visioning process. Some congregations enter into such efforts because they are relatively healthy and excited to move forward together by discerning anew how they might respond to God's call in a new chapter in their ministry. Other congregations are emerging from troubled times—conflict, staff transitions, or concerns for their own survival. Congregations in either situation must seek to answer the questions, Who is God calling us to be and what is God calling us to do in this specific time and place?

At their best, such processes involve prayerful listening and discernment and creative response. The rituals that might be observed as a congregation enters a planning process will differ from one congregation to another based on the situations that led them to this point. The rituals should communicate the need for prayer, listening to God's Spirit, and responding with creative thinking and action.

One ritual might use as symbols the four basic elements of life— earth, fire, water, and wind. The earth symbolized the basic roots and traditions of the congregation. Fire suggests the unique gifts of the congregation's members, both individually and communally, and encourages them to listen to their deepest passion and energy. Fire is a reminder of Pentecost! Water symbolizes new life in God and the need to be a continual moving stream, rather than stuck. The wind represents the need to listen attentively to the Holy Spirit during the entire discernment and planning process and to continue to ask, Where is the Holy Spirit calling us at this point in our communal journey of faith and ministry?

The service might begin with a festive procession of brightly colored banners, each representing one of the four elements. Or the symbols might be represented by a large bag or pot of earth, a burning candle, a jug of water, and a white or silver fan or bright red balloon. A good opening hymn that includes all these symbols is "Spirit of God, Unleashed on Earth."[7] Other appropriate hymns for use in the service might be "Here I Am, Lord," "O Christ, the Great Foundation," "Spirit, Spirit of Gentleness," "Come, O Spirit, Come," "Great God of All the Ages," or "Wind Who Makes All Winds that Called," "Come, O Spirit, Dwell Among Us," "Spirit of the Living God," and "We Are Called."[9]

A litany could be written that incorporates each of the elemental symbols and ties them with the upcoming planning process.

In congregations accustomed to liturgical dance, dancers might carry the four symbols as the interpretation of the hymn texts already suggested or another hymn, such as "Creative God, Your Fingers Trace," "Morning Has Broken," or "God, You Spin the Whirling Planets"[10] to emphasize that God continues to create in this world by inspiring our own creative action as people in communion with one another.

If possible, the congregation then enters into a quiet time. No words are spoken, and no music is played or sung. Worshipers focus only on attentive listening, as they will during the discernment and planning process. If you do choose to have some sound in the background, use a tape or CD of natural sounds—wind blowing or waves lapping or a stream running. Invite the assembly to listen in silent prayer and meditation.

Members of the strategic planning or visioning committee, whether the congregation's regular governance group or a special task force, should be commissioned during the service. At the conclusion of the commissioning, invite congregants to extend a hand toward the planning team and sing a blessing over them. Then a representative of the planning group would ask the entire congregation to covenant to pray daily for the planning process. The congregation should give verbal affirmation of their promise to pray.

As people either enter or leave the service, they might be given a button that includes the theme for the discernment and planning process and the images of the four elements. People should be encouraged to wear the button for congregational events in the coming weeks. Posters with the same words and images might be placed around the church building.

Transition in Norms of Congregations

Sometimes the issue of congregational norms is addressed as part of a strategic planning effort. Other times norms are addressed when the congregation is calling a new pastor or resolving major conflict in the congregation. In any case, a ritual for such a situation is usually best led by a trained facilitator who is not a member of the congregation. Sometimes it will occur at a leadership retreat or at a large congregational meeting. The facilitator begins by explaining the meaning of norms—

the unwritten, psychological rules that govern behavior in a group. Congregations might have norms about aspects of the congregation's life such as children, gender roles, how conflict is handled, building use, member expectations, money, treatment of clergy and staff, role of laity, expectations regarding the clergyperson's family, expectations of visitors or new members, and who is welcome in the congregation.

Divide the participants into small groups (four to six people) and assign one aspect of community life listed above to each group. The groups spend 30 minutes listing on newsprint the norms that are followed in the part of congregational life they are addressing. When the groups have completed their task, each group presents its list of norms. Members of other small groups can suggest additional norms for any list or ask clarifying questions. After all groups have reported, discussion follows regarding which norms serve the congregation well and which norms might no longer serve a good purpose.

The total group might reach consensus on several key norms that are a real gift to the vibrant life of the congregation and several that no longer serve a healthy purpose. Key words summarizing those that are "gifts of life" are written on gift tags attached to attractively wrapped gift packages and brought to an altar or small table that is covered with a cloth and on which sits a lit candle. Key words for those that are no longer seen as serving the congregation's life are written on slips of paper, placed in a large urn, and burned. The facilitator of the gathering leads a prayer written in litany style that affirms norms that have served the congregation well in the past but no longer meet the needs of the church, as well as those that continue to be life-giving. The prayer also asks forgiveness for maintaining norms that perhaps have never represented the church at its best. A concluding hymn such as "Let Us Talents and Tongues Employ," "We Are All One in Mission," or "You Are the Seed"[11] would be an appropriate closing.

A team of representatives chosen from the assembly is then commissioned to meet with the church board and other groups of the church to begin work on changing the norms that were identified as no longer serving the congregation's life and ministry in helpful ways.

Terminating a Congregational Ministry or Program

So often church programs wane and die a slow death, leaving people disappointed or even bitter about the ending. Instead, we might hold a dignified celebration for the life and ministry that took place through that program. A traditional ministry coming to an end in many congregations is the women's or men's group, which is now attended by only a few elderly people. Many groups have given up trying to involve younger men or women who seem to have neither the time nor inclination to participate in such groups. Your congregation might need to celebrate the closure of a chapter of a traditional women's group that has met on a weekday morning once a month for decades. Meetings have included socializing over coffee, a program, plus occasional work projects, such as making quilts for overseas orphanages. A dinner and celebration could be planned for those who are still active in the group. In addition, women who were once part of the group but have moved or left the group could be invited back for this celebration of a ministry that once was a vibrant part of the congregation's life. The younger women of the congregation should be encouraged to attend and applaud contributions this traditional ministry has made to the church.

Following the dinner, string twenty feet of newsprint along one wall. Invite a staff or lay leader with strong process skills to facilitate a time of historical reflection on the life and ministry of this group over the years. Begin with the present and then go backward over the years. After about 30 to 45 minutes of group reflection, divide the participants into small groups to reflect on what for them has been most important about this group. Ensure that each group includes both older and younger women. After about 20 minutes, invite each group to report its observations. You will find these reports are often poignant and include heartwarming and heartwrenching stories. Nearly everyone present will be surprised and elated by all the things this group of women were able to accomplish over the years, the support they have provided to each other, and the difference they have made in the lives of individuals and the congregation.

A worship leader then leads the group in a closing. A litany might be written for the occasion. It could honor the people involved and give thanks for their openness to being led by the Spirit throughout these years, and recognize that in this temporal life, nothing is permanent, save God alone, and that we all need to relinquish things that were dear to us and move on. If the group has often sung certain hymns or songs, these could be sung at this time in the celebration.

Finally, those present should gather in a large double circle, with the people forming the inner circle facing those forming the outer circle. If people seem comfortable doing so, each person could place her right arm on the shoulder of the person to her right and her left arm on the shoulder of the person she is facing in the other circle. The worship leader might suggest a simple one- or two-line mutual blessing that the women could share with each other, such as "Let us give thanks for our friendship together, the ministry we have shared, and bless each other in the next steps of our journey." Finally, close with a single verse of a parting hymn everyone will know by heart, such as the doxology.

Alternatively, the women might chant on one note the word *shalom*, the Hebrew word for "peace." The women do not need to chant in unison. When one runs out of breath, she takes another deep breath and sings it again. This is another form of blessing one another. Other groups might be more comfortable with simply sharing a gesture of peace, such as a hug or handshake, as is done in many congregations during Sunday worship services.

A symbol of the ministry of the group might be given to all who have been members of the group over the years. This could be a certificate, a specially made pin, a coffee mug with an inscription, or some other memento. And finally, the evening could be concluded with a fancy dessert of some kind, such as a lovely cake decorated with symbols of the group's ministry over the years or with the names of members.

Rituals for Clergy Transitions

Leave Taking

Many clergy diminish their ministry in a congregation by neglecting to say good-bye to the congregation as they are leaving. Some individual good-byes will also need to be said to congregational members, such as the elderly or homebound, who might have come to rely deeply on the pastor's ongoing ministry in that church. These members are sometimes hurt when a pastor simply ignores the ending of his or her ministry with them. A number of books have been written about closure processes and rituals for clergy leaving a church, such as *Saying Goodbye*, by church consultant Ed White, or *Running Through the Thistles*, which I authored.[12]

In one congregation, after the last Sunday service at which he presided, the pastor turned over his beeper to another staff member as a humorous symbol of his leaving. A writer in the congregation interviewed several parishioners of different ages and wrote a send-off that affirmed the contributions of the pastor and how members had experienced his presence among them. At the conclusion of the service, members came forward and gathered around the altar as the pastor removed his vestments. They extended their hands in blessing as they sang a closing benediction over him. The pastor, wearing his street clothes, then walked to the back of the church and remained to receive the individual greetings of members.[13]

Waiting for a New Clergyperson

Whether or not an interim pastor works with the congregation between settled pastorates, this time of waiting for a new pastor can be stressful for members of a congregation. Conducting waiting rituals over a period of months can better ensure that the members of the church have done their grieving and that the search committee is given plenty of time to do its ministry of securing a new clergy leader who will be a good fit with the congregation.

A number of scripture passages emphasize the time of waiting: Israel waited for decades in anticipation of the coming of the messiah. Many of the psalms are about waiting, and throughout the psalms, we encounter the lament, "How long, O Lord!" Simeon and Anna await the coming of the one who will deliver the people (Luke 2:25-38). Elizabeth and Mary await the births of their sons, John the Baptist and Jesus (Luke 1:5-2:7).

Rituals of waiting would include prayers that God would send the congregation an appropriate pastor. This ritual might be done in the assembly. Or small groups might be formed in the nave or by having people in every other pew stand and turn around to face those in the pew behind them, and then individuals in the small groups could offer prayers. On some Sunday, the entire worship assembly might be invited to observe a moment of silence as every member consciously prays for the guidance of the Holy Spirit both to assist them in the selection of a new leader and to give them the gift of patient waiting. A hymn about waiting or a significant aspect of the congregation's ministry could be sung each Sunday until the new pastor is selected. Each time it was sung, it would bring awareness of our vulnerability and the need for us to depend on the Holy Spirit during this time of waiting. Some congregations might choose to leave vacant the chair where the lead pastor normally sits during worship. Alternatively, the chair might be removed or placed upside down.

Beginning a New Pastorate

A simple ritual should occur during the first service conducted by the new pastor. It would begin by the pastor putting on his or her robe and stole at the rear of the church as the congregation turns to the back of the church and waits for him or her to enter. At an appropriate time during the service, the specific symbols of the pastor's role and office would be presented, investing in that new pastor the symbols of authority needed to carry out this ministry. Selected members of the congregation representing different age groups would come down the aisle one at a time to present these symbols, such as the pulpit Bible, communion vessels, home communion set, a flask of oil for anointing during healing services, and a glass of water representing ministry to those who thirst spiritually, and perhaps keys to the building. To add a touch of humor, representatives might also present a bottle of aspirin for the many headaches the new pastor will experience in the course of serving the congregation. A lay leader could comment on each of the symbols as they are brought forward. At this point or at the conclusion of the service, the people might extend their hands in blessing as they commission the pastor into ministry at their church, or sing the benediction.

Representatives of the congregation might also wish to bless the home into which the new pastor moves. And likely the members of the church will host a welcoming dinner for the pastor and his or her family. Following the dinner, a series of skits called "This Is Us" might be presented to convey some of the history and character of the congregation and its ministries.

Rituals for Congregations in Conflict

One of the most difficult times in congregational life comes in the confusing and painful time before major conflict is resolved. The following ritual is suggested when a congregation is aware of the conflict and feels stuck. When there are clearly defined sides to an issue and those involved are at enmity with one another, this ritual is best done with the whole congregation during a regular worship service. In more intense levels of conflict when people are so angry with one another that it is difficult to predict what might happen when the individuals or groups are in the same room, the rituals should be structured in a way that allows everyone to maintain some dignity.

Begin with a general prayer of confession led by the congregation's established ritual leader. This confession will not mention specific shortcomings or issues. Following the confession, the words of absolution are offered according to the worshiping community's normal tradition. (When the pastor is identified as being a member of one of the camps in the conflict, this prayer might be led by another worship leader who is perceived to be neutral.)

The third party working with the congregation to manage the conflict then briefly describes where the congregation is in the conflict resolution process. (If no consultant or arbitrator is serving the congregation, this would likely be done by the worship leader or a skilled facilitator from within the congregation.) This person will state the main issues, what steps have been taken to date to confront these concerns, and how the process appears to be stuck at the present time. She or he reminds congregants that throughout history and in biblical times, other groups have confronted such situations but through perseverance were able to work through their issues and remain related to one another. The facilitator asks the people to identify biblical or historical accounts of people who were seemingly stuck in conflict but persevered and succeeded in restoring their relationship.

Following this sharing time, the members of the assembly are invited to pray aloud or silently for their congregation—for the ability to persevere and speak in ways that can be heard and understood by others, and to understand those whose perspectives differ from their own. The congregation would then proceed with the remainder of the worship service.

Once conflict has reached a clear resolution, other rituals might be employed. In a small congregation, this ritual could be part of the regular

Sunday worship service, whereas a large congregation might conduct the ritual in an informal gathering created so those involved in the conflict might gather for sharing and worship.

Invite members of the various factions to share their sense of the resolution that has been accomplished and their gratitude for the aspect of this resolution they most value. The ritual leader then leads the group through a confession of sins that can deepen the sense of resolution that has been achieved. Participants are invited to confess ways in which they think they contributed to the conflict, either by what they did or said or by what they neglected to do or say. Each speaker focuses on his or her own behavior and not that of anyone else.

After all who wish have shared their confessions, the worship leader offers the words of absolution. The leader neither asks members to forgive one another nor tells them they are reconciled. Members will do that in their own way in their own time. The ritual is then followed by a time of refreshments during which people who wish can privately say more to one another in a spirit of reconciliation.[14]

Other Transition Rituals in Congregations

• *Ritual for those joining the congregation*: Most denominations have a set liturgy or worship format for receiving new members. The danger with such rituals is that they can become predictable. A welcoming ritual with some real gusto might better convey the joy of joining a vigorous congregation and engaging in its mission. A song might be written for the occasion. New members would face the congregation as the congregants sing them this song of joy and welcome. If this song is lively and members become used to welcoming newcomers in this way, they will be able to sing it with exuberance. Following the service, a reception would be held to celebrate the occasion. Each individual or family joining the congregation would be hosted by two people or a couple who would introduce them to several other people. In this way, individual members can also offer a welcome.

• *Rituals for members leaving the congregation*: The individual or family members leaving the congregation are invited to come forward. Someone briefly reviews their history with the congregation and the contributions they have made. (A written letter might also affirm the special gifts they have brought to the congregation.) The departing member or family is commissioned as evangelists from this congregation. Alternatively, a congregation might gives the member(s) leaving the congregation a hymnal. Other members of the congregation could choose their favorite hymn in the hymnal and on that page write their comments and appreciation for the person or family. The hymnal is then presented during the worship service. (When possible it is also helpful to have exit interviews conducted with those leaving the church.)

• *Staff member leaving on sabbatical*: This ritual might best take place at the conclusion of a Sunday worship service. Before the closing hymn, leaders of the congregation should come forward, either face or surround the staff member, and, with a litany, commission the one leaving on sabbatical, asking that person be granted physical, emotional, intellectual and spiritual renewal. The staff member then might hand to the leaders one or more symbols of the ministry responsibility he or she normally carries—the pastor, a stole; the director of religious education, perhaps a Bible or church school curriculum; a music leader, a score or hymnal; and so forth. This symbol might be placed in a prominent place in the sanctuary or other gathering place as a reminder to the members of the congregation to pray for the staff member while he or she remains on renewal leave. The one leaving on sabbatical can also covenant to pray for the congregation during this time away. Facing the congregation, the staff member would receive the blessing of members of the congregation who extend their arms in a blessing gesture toward him or her. The staff member then would process from the sanctuary and, at the back of the church or during a coffee hour, receive the greetings and best wishes of individual members.

• *Staff member returning from sabbatical*: When the staff member returns from sabbatical leave, a similar ritual is performed. Instead of taking place at the end of the service, however, it occurs at the beginning of the service. After the first hymn, the leaders of the congregation would call forth the returning staff member. Whatever symbol had been surrendered at the time of the sabbatical leave-taking would be returned, and a prayer of welcoming return would be offered by a lay leader. The staff member would have a brief opportunity to thank the congregation for their prayers and share what the time of renewal meant to him or her. After singing a festive hymn, the worship service would continue.

• *Beginning small group or committee meetings at the church*: A number of rituals are available to begin such gatherings. Balancing traditional and new rituals might best serve groups. A candle might be lit and then prayer offered. In small groups, members might do a quick check-in using a formula such as "Tonight I feel _____ because _____." Other simple community-building exercises might be used to help members to get to know one another at a deeper level. A sentence-completion exercise can assist members to reflect on their gifts, life experiences, passions and dreams.[15] Or the group might engage in in-depth reflection on a topic related to their ministry. For example, members of a group working on the children's education program might briefly describe an outstanding teacher they once had. Or members developing the capital fund drive might consider talk about a time in life when something thought to be impossible happened.[16] Alternatively, members might be asked to bring something that symbolizes a personal gift they want to share in the committee or a symbol for the committee's own ministry. Each group members might name a favorite hymn or prayer or scripture passage that symbolizes their work and ministry.

• *Concluding a small group or committee meeting*: Quality rituals for closing meetings are important in order to cement the positive experiences in the meeting and to redeem some of the negative ones. When members simply rush for the door as the last agenda item is concluded, the impression (and likely reality) is that no one wanted to be at the gathering in the first place. Part of the closure ritual will normally include a brief period for reflection and evaluation about both the content of the meeting and the quality of the processes used and relationships experienced. When the meeting agenda is being designed, time should be allotted for this process, so it is experienced as integral to the meeting and not just an add on. Either the chairperson or a designated facilitator might simply ask, "What did you like about the way we worked together this evenings, and what concerns you about the way we did our ministry together tonight?" Sometimes this is called a "celebration and concerns" process. Participants' comments can address both tasks and relationships. Groups might establish some traditions about these evaluation and reflection times, or they might use a variety of processes. An occasional alternative might be to conclude with group members expressing gratitude for aspects of their ministry and relationships or affirming specific gifts and contributions of each group member.

To set a prayerful environment conducive to discernment, the candle used during the group's opening ritual might be relit when this reflection occurs. Many groups like to conclude the evaluation with the Lord's Prayer, the sharing of a gesture of peace, and perhaps singing together a hymn about mission, calling or gratitude. Possible hymns might include: "We Are Called," "Lord, You Give the Great Commission," or "Let Us Talents and Tongues Employ."[17]

Other Opportunities for Ritualizing Transitions

- Consecrating new office space, office equipment, building furnishings
- Beginning new ministry programs
- Beginning or concluding a building program
- Installing new lay leaders
- Sending members into the mission field as volunteers or staff members
- Sending young people or adults on service trips
- Seeking physical or emotional healing
- Celebrating a ministry in progress
- Commissioning lay ministry groups
- Developing a new mission or vision statement for congregation

Reflection Exercises

1. In a gathering of your family or a small group at church, identify several of the transition points within the life of your faith community during the past five years. Recall how they were ritualized. What transitions are you anticipating in the months ahead? How might these provide opportunities for meaningful ritual to honor the transition? How might you suggest or help plan such a ritual?

2. Invite a group of young people in the confirmation class, youth group, or church school to create a ritual for one of the transitions listed under "Other Opportunities for Ritualizing Transitions." Encourage the young people to plan and lead the rituals they create.

3. Ask several groups within the church to brainstorm opportunities for ritualizing transitions in the lives of congregational members. Encourage groups to provide feedback on which rituals described in this chapter would be most meaningful to them.

4. As part of the training of church school teachers and pastoral care lay ministers, discuss the role of ritual in the life of children and youth as well as for the ill and those in crisis. Encourage each group to create and implement at least one ritual for those with whom they minister.

CHAPTER 5

The Public Role of Congregations

Today, more than ever, we need community rituals that bring together
the rich diversity in our communities and assist people to acknowledge the changes that are taking place in our neighborhoods and the
larger culture. Ritualizing cultural and community transitions allows
us to give meaning and shape to what is transpiring among us, leaves
us feeling less like victims of change, and allows us to bond with people
of different religious and ethnic traditions, races, and socioeconomic
backgrounds. Through ritual we can acknowledge our common experiences related to these transitions. Communities benefit from ritual
when, in the midst of accelerating change, society in general is becoming more isolated and fragmented.

Rituals have the capacity to unite diverse communities, because
rituals use symbols that can carry meaning across racial, ethnic, religious, gender, and age boundaries. We see perhaps the most dramatic
examples of effective communication through symbol when throughout entire nations or even across the globe, people of all backgrounds
and walks of life engage in spontaneous rituals marking the death of a
public figure. Flowers and tokens are brought by thousands to various
central sites, people sign condolence books, families and strangers
gather around televisions and flock to local memorial services to express their grief. In less dramatic circumstances, people gather at community parks for a Fourth of July fireworks display and at neighborhood churches for ecumenical Thanksgiving services. We have also
become accustomed to people of all races celebrating Martin Luther
King Jr. Day with worship services, educational events, marches, and
other remembrances.

Whether the community gathers to recognize a national holiday

or to plant a tree in a neighborhood park in memory of those who have
died in a natural disaster or human-made tragedy, rituals have the potential to bring completeness to certain aspects of life. They unite us in
a spirit of oneness, offer an avenue for expressing our feelings, and
broaden our perspective on life-changing events. They help us to view
all of life—with all its blessedness and all its tragedy.

Regular Rituals in the Community

Perhaps your congregation has frequently played a role in certain public holiday rituals and services such as those discussed above. Or maybe
your clergyperson has participated in the dedication of a public building. You will likely wish to continue these traditional types of involvement in public ritualizing. There might be other opportunities to create
public rituals, however, not just for transitional times in the community
but on a predictable basis.

Blessing of the Animals

A growing number of congregations, for example, hold services for
the blessing of animals. Members of the larger community as well as
of the congregation itself are invited to bring their pets for the blessing.
The main theme of the service is the wonder of creation and our call to
live in harmony with nature. The service can be held either indoor or
outdoors and might include a procession of the animals (St. John the
Divine Episcopal Cathedral in New York City even has an elephant in
its procession), hymns such as "All Things Bright and Beautiful,"[1] scripture readings such Genesis 1:20-26 and Psalm 148:7-14, responsive
readings, and the Prayer of St. Francis. The ritual typically includes a
blessing of the animals and the individuals or families who care for
them. Those performing the blessing use the pet's name and note the
special joy this animal brings to this family as well as the loving environment the owners provide for the pets. The offering that day might
be distributed to an animal shelter or the Humane Society. These rituals remind us that as human beings, we are among the earth's many
creatures, all of whom are loved creations of God. (See appendix E on
page 139 for a sample ritual.)

Cleaning Up Public Lands

It is not uncommon for youngsters, teens, and adults to gather for community cleanup days. The effort might involve cleaning roadsides, a community park, riverbanks, or a vacant lot. Such activities might be made even more meaningful if they began and ended with short rituals. A ritual would remind everyone that we share responsibility for the care of the earth and for keeping our neighborhoods and rural lands clean and safe for all to enjoy.

As people gather with tools and garbage bags, they might stand in a large circle and observe a moment of silence and then sing the chant "The Earth Is Our Mother, We Must Take Care of Her"[2] or another environmental song. A communal prayer or litany might note the themes that working together is a blessing and that the day's work begins in a spirit of joy and gratefulness. Each worker could then be given a button or ribbon to wear with a symbol of the clean-up or restoration effort.

At the conclusion of the work time, a special ceremony might be held to plant a new tree, shrub, or small bed of flowers, or to erect a sign or other reminder of both the beauty of the earth and the joy community residents experience when they join to care for their neighborhood and the earth. If a planting is done, several buckets of water might be placed nearby, and workers could be invited to cup water with their hands and pour it onto the tree or flower bed. Finally, the group might circle round their planting and join again in the chant before closing by offering each other high fives, smiles, and thanks for work well done together.

Annual Festival of Faiths

An annual Festival of Faiths is held in Louisville, Kentucky each year.[3] This five-day festival showcases through booths and activities the contributions of various religious groups to the larger community—groups as diverse as the Ursuline Sisters; local Protestant, Roman Catholic, and Greek Orthodox congregations; the Salvation Army; and Hindu, Islamic, and Buddhist organizations. Participants explore special themes, talk about their diverse beliefs and practices, and listen to special speakers and educational events. An annual interfaith Thanksgiving service occurs during the festival and is participated in by both the religious community and prominent civic leaders. A gala dinner and celebration follows the service.

Louisville's interfaith efforts have a long tradition but are "a concept ripe for transplantation. The idea of helping cities see their religious roots and their religious selves, of helping create conversations where there was only silence or bigotry is a very large and good one."[4]

Ritual to Address Hunger

Congregations commonly participate in ongoing outreach ministry by contributing to a community food shelf or pantry. Though we live in hope, we realize that hunger will likely need to be addressed both locally and globally for years to come. It is essential that we maintain our staying power as individuals, congregations, and communities to provide food for the hungry. An annual ritual might increase the bond among people and congregations involved in this effort, recognize the meaning of their important shared ministry, and celebrate the community's solidarity with those in need. This ritual celebration would likely be conducted at a local food shelf or at a central location representing a coalition of several such food pantries, or it could be held in conjunction with another gathering of an interfaith coalition. Participants would be invited to bring canned food and perhaps a symbol of their congregation or organization, such as a banner. The invocation would focus on our call to feed the hungry, our gratitude for our abundant blessings, and our solidarity with our hungry brothers and sisters in the community. Prayers would remind us of a compassionate God who offers each of us bread and calls us to feed the multitudes not out of obligation but from generous hearts and a deep belief that we are one humanity. Scripture readings could include Deuteronomy 10:17-19, Luke 9:10-17, and Matthew 25:31-46. In community rituals that are not only ecumenical but interfaith, it will be important to include leaders, readings, and prayers from the traditions of the community participants, perhaps including Jews, Buddhists, Hindus, Native Americans, or others.

The ritual leader and several assistants then pick up large baskets and go to each person in the room and ask, "Do you covenant to continue in this ministry of feeding the hungry?" The person places a food item in the basket and responds, "Yes, by the help of God." The service concludes with a closing prayer and benediction or a hymn such as "Whatsoever You Do to the Least of My Brethren"[5] or "Gift of Finest Wheat."[6]

Transition Rituals

Just as individuals, families, and congregations use ritual to make meaning of life transitions, so too communities can ritualize endings, the neutral time of waiting and confusion, and new beginnings. Several specific rituals are outlined below. Each, of course, can be adapted in many ways.

Waiting through Drought or Flood

It is not uncommon for one part of our continent to be experiencing great drought while another area is recovering from severe flooding. These times as well as the rituals we use to observe them remind us of the importance of water and how often we take this life-sustaining substance for granted. Indeed, water is part of our very essence. It covers 70 percent of the earth's surface and makes up 65 percent of our own bodies. Yet the ways and times in which it comes to us are usually out of our control. Few experiences can make human beings feel more powerless than the extremes of drought and of flooding. Both experiences require our supreme patience and hope in the future.

Drought. Community members gather at a location where the effects of drought are obvious, such as in a parched field of dry and cracked soil and severely damaged crops. Standing in a circle, people describe in a few words the effect the drought has had on them and their families. For some people, the drought brings severe financial loss; for others, the loss is psychological—living without the joy of bright flowers, green grass, and succulent shrubbery or watching the leaves of trees wither and die. Children miss playing in backyard swimming pools. Perhaps urban dwellers are inconvenienced by water rationing. At the end of this sharing, participants offer prayers in a sentence or two.

The ritual leader invites participants to hold out the palms of their hands and then places a few drops of water in each person's palm. Participants say aloud some of the reasons they appreciate water, and then all swallow the water from their hand. In closing, each is asked to share a commitment they have made to change their lifestyle so as not to waste water in the future, even when the land is not in drought. To each person's commitment, others respond, "For your water, we thank you, Lord." As a closing benediction, the ritual leader dips an evergreen branch in a basin of water and gives everyone a light sprinkle of water with the words, "May the God who created the wonder of water bless and keep you." or "May fresh, clean water bless you all the days of your life." The group could conclude with the hymn "Be Not Afraid" or "O Healing River."[7]

Flooding. Participants gather in rain gear near the edge of flood waters. The ritual begins with a simple chant about water. One such chant has the following words:

> The river is flowing,
> Flowing and growing.
> The river is flowing back to the sea.
> Mother, carry me
> Child I will always be
> Mother carry me back to the sea.[8]

The ritual leader then offers an opening prayer, such as the following:

> Lord, through Noah you promised humankind that you would
> never again destroy the earth with a flood, and you gave us
> the sign of the rainbow as assurance of that promise. We are
> gathered here today very much in need of a rainbow—some
> assurance from you that our lives will not be destroyed by
> flood waters. We ask this in your holy name. Amen

A music leader begins singing "Our God, Our Help in Ages Past."[9] In small groups, participants then talk briefly about the effect of the flood on their lives and that of their families. Such sharing serves a therapeutic purpose, because stress will be high among people. After returning to the large group, the ritual leader emphasizes the value and necessity of water and points out that we do not control the timing of either floods or drought but must somehow float above the stress that such events bring to our lives.

Short pieces of dowelling are handed out to participants, and each person is asked to write his or her name on the piece of wood and toss it into a tub of water (or series of tubs, if a large number of people are participating). The people join hands and offer spontaneous prayer of support for one another. Then in a symbolic gesture of mutual support, each person removes from the washtub a piece of wood with another name on it. The ritual leader concludes with a prayer such as the following:

> Gracious God, teach us how to be like wood. No matter how high the flood water rises, we will be able to float above it. And so we close this prayer time with those ancient words you have taught us to pray: Our Father, who art in heaven ...

Then the entire group of people sings together a hymn such as "Michael Row the Boat Ashore."[10] As participants leave the site, they might be given pins with rainbows on them to place on their lapels, or they might share a sign of peace with one another.

Renovation of a Home for a Homeless Family

The ritual begins as volunteer or paid workers, neighbors, and members of supporting groups gather in front of the house that is to be or has been refurbished. An invocation and prayers acknowledge the trials of homelessness and the difference a permanent place of residence can make in the life of a family. The home is offered to the service of God and neighbor, and the home is blessed to be a place of shelter, safety, growth, and laughter. Prayers of gratitude are offered for those who have worked to renovate the home and support the efforts financially.

Incense is placed in a censor or heavy dish, and people follow the ritual leader throughout the home to its major rooms. In each room, the censor is swung to all four corners of the room, or the dish is extended toward each corner, as the leader recites the opening of Psalm 141:2: "Let [our] prayer be counted as incense before you." The people respond, "And the lifting up of [our] hands as an evening sacrifice." As they respond, they extend their arms in blessing. In each room, a different prayer might be offered following this ritual blessing:

In the living room: "May this room be a place of hospitality and nurture for friends and family."

In the kitchen: "May the joyful preparation of healthy food fill this room each day."

In the dining room: "May nutritious food be eaten here with joy amid loving conversation."

In the bedrooms: "May this room be a place of peaceful and healing rest for all who bring here their weariness and need for healing."

Finally, all process to the entrance hallway: "May peace abide with all who enter this place. May love be both offered and received while they remain."

Those present are encouraged to respond to each prayer with the phrase "Thanks be to God."

At the conclusion of the ritual, light refreshments might be served on the front lawn or inside the home as an expression of the hospitality that will be experienced by a new family in the home. (A similar ritual might be designed for anyone moving into a new dwelling place. Friends and new neighbors could be invited to join in such a house blessing.)

Community Rituals Acknowledging Violent Deaths

In the city of Indianapolis, the Church Federation of Greater Indianapolis has formed a prayer vigil network of people who conduct a brief ritual on each site in the city where a violent death has occurred. The network's mission is shared at the beginning of every liturgy they conduct:

> By gathering for a brief prayer vigil we will stand in solidarity with our brothers and sisters against that which destroys our city by destroying its citizens. Whenever someone is killed we all are affected.[11]

Several symbolic actions take place during the vigil liturgy. While scripture is read, the ground or pavement where the death occurred is anointed with oil as a symbol of healing in that place. In addition, a "peace pole" that has the names of all the people who have died a violent death in that city is brought to the site. Twice a year the federation also holds a community remembrance service for all people who have died within the previous six months. People who knew a victim come forward to light a candle at the service. Such services are held in different congregations. Those who support this ritual ministry call themselves the Sanctuary Church Movement. The movement has also developed a mentoring program in collaboration with local hospitals. Mentors are trained to provide support for victims' families. This interfaith movement has grown to include a phone tree of over 300 names. Whenever the early morning rituals are scheduled, the phone tree is used to contact members with the information about time, place, and who has been killed.

When there is an act of violence in the wider world, the movement sometimes conducts similar rituals, because they recognize that members of their local community are personally affected as well. In this way, the community acknowledges the common bond among all people of the world.

Farm Closing

For the past two decades, we have seen the steady erosion of small family-owned farms across America. My wife, Carole, grew up on such a farm near Hershey, Pennsylvania, and experienced the agony of watching this family farm be sold to a developer who planned to build houses on the property. She is very clear that she would have appreciated a closure ritual at the old farmhouse—a ritual that would have included members of her congregation as well as her neighbors and friends. It might have been designed something like this:

As people gather at the farm, they would recall the many times the congregation had prepared for their annual chicken and corn soup suppers on that site. (Volunteers from the church prepared soup in forty-gallon cooking pots at the farm, spending the better part of a weekend preparing for this event. Neighbors from miles around attended the supper.) At the farm closing ritual, these and other memories and stories would be shared. Those who remember when the farm was in full operation would provide the history of the farm—the eras when peach orchards grew on the land and when the farm later emphasized its dairy operation and eventually cash crops. Neighbors and family members could provide the story of the rich farming tradition on this land from the 1940s through the early 1980s.

Following the retelling of the history of the farm, a hymn of thanksgiving would be sung. Over the years the land had produced thousands of tons of food for the public, so the hymn would be one of gratitude for the way in which the land provided health and nourishment for thousands of people. A prayer would acknowledge that although the land was now changing ownership and would be used and cared for in a different way, the beauty of its trees and rolling hills might still be appreciated and sustained.

Those participating in the ritual would gather around the big barn and each place their hands on it, then circle the barn in a procession as a thanksgiving hymn was sung. A prayer of thanks would be offered for the ways the barn had served: as a shelter for farm animals and a storage place for hay and corn, as well as a milking station during the years the farm raised dairy cows. The people would face the barn and raise their hands in blessing over it. The friends and neighbors would then process to the farmhouse and repeat a similar ritual of song, prayer, and blessing. The farm would then be transferred to the new owner in some symbolic way, such as handing the new owner the keys to the house and a can full of earth. A prayer would be offered for those who would soon occupy the land and manage it in a different way. If possible, a lunch of chicken and corn soup would have be served in the farm yard after the ritual concluded.

Finally, people would walk or drive out the front gate and the gate would be closed, symbolizing the ending of the farm life that had existed there for over a hundred years. A sign might be posted on the gate that read, "We bless you on your way. May you in your new life on this land also reverence this space as holy ground."

Other Community Rituals of Transition

• *Closing of a hospice unit*: When the Health East Hospice Unit at St. Joseph's Hospital in St. Paul, Minnesota, closed, one of the chaplains led about thirty nurses, social workers, volunteers, and other hospice workers through a ritual of closure. The service began with a scripture reading. Participants then viewed part of a video, "The Little Tin Box" by Edward J. Hayes.[12] In accordance with the story told in the video, a small tin box was passed from person to person, and each person present shared a memory, a story about their work in the hospice unit over the years, that they wished to place in the box. For this group of hospice workers, this ritualizing of an ending of an important program in their hospital was a very moving one.

• *Silent Witness Project*: The Silent Witness National Initiative "promotes successful community-based domestic violence reduction efforts in order to reach zero domestic murders by 2010" in the United States.[13] Among its other efforts are Silent Witness Exhibits of near life-size plywood figures representing women killed in domestic violence. One congregation designed plywood figures of women who had been killed in their community. One year they displayed them on posts next to a major highway of their city; another year they set them next to a state route in front of their own newly built church. The congregation also commissioned a musician to write a new song related to domestic violence; the song included some of the names of those women whom the figures represented.[14]

• *Ritual for a new era*: Congregations might provide community rituals for ushering in new periods in our history, whether the new year, the coming decade, a new millennium, or a new era after the accomplishment of some major community goal or recovery from a community disaster. These rituals might occur in the church building, in a public arena, or in small clusters in people's homes. Hymns could be chosen that express confidence in the providence of God throughout all the changes in the world. Individuals of various ages and walks of life could offer brief stories about their hopes for the future. Videos or slides might celebrate the accomplishments of the period of time that is soon drawing to an end.

Just prior to midnight all might light candles and sing an appropriate hymn or song together in the candlelight. Then at the stroke of the clock, all would be invited to extinguish their candles and the room would remain in darkness except for one candle in the front or center of the room. This lone burning candle would symbolize the light of God who remains present with us through all the dark times of our lives. After several moments of silence in the near darkness, someone would light his or her candle from the God candle, and the light would then be passed from person to person until everyone in the room was once again holding a lit candle. The leader might announce the words of Isaiah 9:2: "The people who walked in darkness have seen a great light; those who lived in a land of deep darkness—on them a light has shined," and participants would then share the sign of peace with one other and break bread together as they entered together into a new age, trusting in each other and in the presence of their Creator and Sustainer.

• *Supporting emergency personnel and caregivers in disasters*: Perhaps no one stands in greater need of ritualizing than those emergency personnel and social service and religious community caregivers during and after a natural disaster or human-caused catastrophe. The toll such emergencies place on people in such roles is severe, and the emotional aftermath is often invisible to the larger population.[15] Not only will such people benefit from the availability of ongoing counseling and support and liberal vacation leave and sabbaticals, but community-wide, ecumenical, and interfaith ritual will be helpful as well. These people have been on the front lines providing care and opening the way for healing for others and as a consequence must be offered opportunities for their own healing as well. A ritual service of healing gives these caregivers permission to grieve and to receive nurture from the surrounding communities and from God. (You will find a sample service in appendix G on page 145.)

• *Ritual when war begins*: Often in our history this nation has engaged in wars, and nearly as frequently our people have disagreed about the justness of those military conflicts. Perhaps we can more easily agree on the need for rituals and prayer that acknowledge that we have entered into an action of last resort and should be in prayer for all people involved and for the earth. Such ritual acknowledges that

both we and our perceived enemies are human beings created and
loved by God and that both sides have failed to follow God's way of
love. These rituals might help us avoid becoming anesthetized by the
pictures of the onslaught in newspapers, magazines, and on television
and keep us from demonizing those with whom we are at conflict.

In our rituals and prayer, we might seek forgiveness for not
discovering better ways to resolve our differences, for our lack of
wisdom as members of the human community, for the inevitable kill-
ing of innocent people, and for contributing toward further hatred and
animosity as a result of the violence. At any stage of the conflict, rituals of sorrow and repentance that acknowledge our inability to resolve
our differences peacefully will be appropriate. The rituals might include lament, expressing our grief and sorrow for the tragedy suffered
by both sides in the war. Rather than celebrating our victories in some
jingoistic way, we might better engage in rituals similar to those conducted by ancient warriors who at the end of violent conflicts engaged
in rituals of sorrow and repentance.

• *Ritual for a business layoff or closing*: When a manufacturing plant
or major business is closed, those who have worked there for years as
well as members of the larger community will experience a kind of
death. Not only are there huge financial implications for workers and
community businesses, but familiar and long-standing relationships,
routines, and sources of meaning will have been disrupted. Ritualizing
the closing of a plant or business or a large number of layoffs might
take the form of a funeral or memorial service. Workers, their families,
and members of the surrounding community might gather for a symbolic burial of this place of productivity and employment. A coffinlike
box could be suspended over a hole in the ground, or participants
might be invited to imagine a coffin in their presence.

Several people could be invited to offer short eulogies celebrating
the meaning and life of the business. What made the plant unique?
What will people miss—or not miss? (If only a small group is present,
spontaneous remembrances might be offered.) Once the box is lowered into the ground, the ritual leader picks up some dirt and drops it on
top of the box with the words, "Ashes to ashes, dust to dust. As with all
things in this temporal world, death is a natural part of the wheel of life.
Those that remain need to move on with life. Yet to grieve well is to

open the way for new possibilities." Each person might then add a handful of dirt as they leave. Participants might also be given a memento of the plant.

Other Opportunities for Community Rituals

- Accomplishing a major community goal
- Beginning a collaborative effort by various institutions in the community
- Exercising citizenship responsibilities such as voting
- Encouraging citizens to address issues of justice in the community
- Creating a community garden or farmer's market
- Death of a global, national, or community leader
- Demolition of a community building
- Summer and winter equinox

Reflection Exercises

1. With a group of family or friends, recall times when congregations in your community have been involved in public rituals. Have most of these rituals involved celebrating holidays, acknowledging disasters, or supporting community-wide efforts to strengthen the community?

2. Recall two or three times of transition in the life of your community when you believe your congregation might have aided the community by providing leadership for ritualizing the situation people were experiencing.

3. With a church or community group, or as a family activity, design a ritual for some community issue about which you are concerned, such as the environment, housing, employment, teen activities, safety issues, and so forth. Invite each member of the group to contribute at least one idea for the ritual.

4. Speak with members of your congregation's social outreach or
    social action committee about the possibility of being involved in
    or leading rituals for issues and transitions in community life. In-
    vite the committee members to study this chapter of this book for
    further reference.

5. Talk with friends or neighbors who are not members of your con-
    gregation about their thoughts and feelings about the role ritual
    might play in addressing community concerns. If people seem
    interested, discuss what small steps you might take on your own
    block or immediate neighborhood.

CHAPTER 6

Evaluating Rituals

In order for rituals to have transformative power in our lives, they should fit our theology, lifestyle, biorhythm, and personal style. For example, to fit our theology and belief system, rituals need to support and affirm what we believe about God, ourselves in relationship to God, and what we believe God desires for us. Even within the same denominational traditions, we should not assume that other people work with a theology identical to our own.

A number of issues are involved in matching rituals with lifestyle. We will want to take into account our living situation. If we live with others, it might take some work to create the quiet time and space we need. On the other hand, if we live alone, we might need to make arrangements for people to join us for rituals that work better if they are conducted by a group. Our schedule affects ritual, too. If, for example, we travel a great deal in our work, we need to build time into the days on the road for our personal rituals. If families are to share rituals, they need to choose times that are convenient for all members of the family, taking into consideration work, school, and other activities of the various members of the family.

We need to respect our body's preferences as much as possible, too. Our rituals serve us best if we engage in them when our energy is highest, for example. A ritual late at night is unlikely to work well for a morning person, whereas it would fit a night owl just fine.

The relationship of personal style to ritual preference is considerably more complex. A number of authors have related personality type and learning style to our preferences for prayer and worship practices.[1] Although our personal style preferences might mean we feel greater satisfaction and comfort with certain types of rituals than others, we might actually choose to enter into rituals that go against type, because we want greater integration and balance in our lives. Particularly by midlife, people start to be curious about and grow from exploring "the pieces of their personalities that are not yet developed. They need to move toward their own wholeness."[2]

Even gender and cohort groups will have some influence on ritual preferences. It is likely that a group of men gathering for ritual might select somewhat different symbols, for example, than a group of women. And the pre-World War II generation might be more comfortable with traditional rituals than baby boomers and generation Xers. Generation Xers, on the other hand, might wish to use video or other high-tech visuals in rituals, which an older generation might not even consider.

Of course, when designing rituals for congregational and community groups and even for families, we can assume the group includes people with a variety of personal style preferences, so some balance in ritual design and content will be needed to provide the most meaningful experience for all. By including elements that will appeal to people with different styles, everyone will be called to stretch a little and thus will be invited into the transformation process. Leaders of ritual need to be especially careful, however, that they do not design rituals that reflect only one personal style or preference. Rather than designing rituals for certain personality or learning styles, balance is what is most called for.

The Potential Destructive Side of Ritual

As we have noted throughout this book, ritual has great potential to transform. We should be aware, however, that it can become destructive as well. Because of ritual's deep meaning, our choices of symbols, words, gestures, and other aspects of ritual hold the potential for both good and evil. To ritualize is always to risk. We can employ ritual to help us grow; we can also use it to protect us from the frightening aspects of spiritual growth. We can use ritual to face ourselves and life squarely, or we can use it to avoid looking at ourselves.

Let us consider an extreme example of ritual gone array. The swastika symbols of the Third Reich in Germany, the goose-step marching, and requirement that Jews wear a star of David and have numbers tattooed on their arms in the death camps were rituals destructive not only of Jews but of the entire German culture and its people. In almost any jingoistic regime, powerful symbols and rituals are employed to portray outsiders and foreigners as the enemy and to arouse nationalistic fervor for the cause. It is easy for a citizen of any country to become caught up in all such ritualizing. It is always easier to blame our difficulties on others rather than to look at ourselves or the simple realities of change in our world. Leaders of the Third Reich actually ritualized that blame.

The key way to distinguish between the transformative and the destructive potential of ritual is to use the criterion of love. Love needs to be the end result of all of our ritualizing, whether our rituals are private, family-oriented, or for the congregation or larger community. As cocreators with God, we are able to do incredible things through the genuine love that flows through us. Rituals can enable us to exercise this love in a concrete way. Rituals can allow us to acknowledge with gratitude that love sustains all of us.

Any ritual, however, that lowers our sense of love for self or others needs to be suspect. Rituals that are shaming or that exclude those different from us should be questioned. We should ask whether the ritual makes us a more inclusive and loving person and community or narrows our focus to our own selfish concerns. There are two critical questions to ask about our ritualizing: Do our rituals lead us "toward greater self-esteem, aliveness, wholeness, health, love, and justice" (as spiritually transformative rituals will)? Do they lead us "toward isolation and alienation, fear, prejudice, resignation, and a gradual death of self" (individual or communal)?[3]

Some categories might help you be particularly alert to potentially destructive sides of rituals. Here are a few to consider.[4]

Obligatory Rituals

We want to use ritual to acknowledge and honor individuals and groups in our communities. But we must guard against the tendency to get locked into continuing rituals that have long since lost their meaning and, in fact, might have become a source of simmering anger and resentment. For example, perhaps Christmas Eve has come to mean going to a grandparent's house, where a large segment of the family drinks too much and subsequently gets into fights. Yet because family members feel obligated to be part of the gathering, no one dares to say they will not participate in this scene anymore. Or major holidays might mean preparing an enormous Christmas Eve dinner and opening Christmas gifts with family at your home, then rushing to a Christmas brunch and opening stockings at another family members' home, and then dashing to a third family member's place for more festivities and another large meal on Christmas night. Year after year, everyone is exhausted, but no one suggests that the entire family sit down and reach consensus on a simpler and less hectic Christmas for everyone.

Women especially often feel heavy expectations about rituals at holiday times. The cultural expectations are that they will plan and prepare for family celebrations, shop for food and presents, send cards, prepare the meals, and make sure everyone is invited and has a good time. Increasingly, such expectations cause great tension in many families.

When rituals are obligatory, participants celebrate them more out of that feeling of obligation than because of any sense of meaning. Both the preparation process and the ritual itself are more burden than joy. Obligatory rituals often leave little room for spontaneity or playfulness and are generally experienced as stressful by participants. Some people might even feel fear and anxiety if they consider trying to change these rituals, and they experience both guilt and rejection if they do opt out of them.

To explore whether you feel locked into obligatory rituals, some basic questions might be helpful. Think of the major rituals in your family over the last few years. Then recall traditional congregational rituals and perhaps some community-wide ones as well.

- Do you look forward to them, or does their approach fill you with a sense of burden and dread?
- After a ritual is over, do you feel some sense of satisfaction and renewal of relationships, or do you just feel relieved that this event is over for another year?
- If you are quite dissatisfied with a given ritual, is your family, friendship group, congregation, or community group willing to discuss the matter, or will you be given the shaming message that you need to "get back into line."

Rigid Rituals

We want to acknowledge the sense of security and groundedness that comes from doing rituals the same way over a long period of time. Most of us like some traditions. There is always the danger of overemphasizing this aspect of ritual, however. When rituals become rigid, they constrain individual expression and ongoing development. In some families and church groups, for example, nearly all the behavior and symbols in a given ritual are highly prescribed and unvaried over many years. The ritual must occur exactly the same way today as it did yesterday or precisely the same way this year as last. There is almost no room for anything new or spontaneous to occur. Playfulness and humor are totally absent. Often such rituals originate from a protective motive. They may provide a way to thwart feelings of anxiety, grief, or fear.

For example, after a particularly popular leader or staff member has died or for some other reason left a church or a specific ministry program, members might insist on celebrating an event just the way that previous leader did, even though the leader has been gone for months, if not years. Rigidity about rituals that occur either during or after a traumatic event or crisis might be a signal that someone—you, the family, or the group—is having trouble coping with an especially frightening transition.

To be alert for rigid rituals, you might ask the following questions:

- Would I (we) feel anxious if we tried this ritual in a way different from the way we have done it before? What would happen if we chose to let ourselves really experience this anxiety and see what it has to teach us?
- Would we feel uncomfortable if someone suggested beforehand that we change the ritual or spontaneously introduced something novel during the ritual?
- When was the last time we changed anything about this ritual or ceremony?

Minimized Rituals

In some groups, including family groups and neighborhoods, there are almost no recognizable rituals at all. Significant events and transitions in these groups are ignored or only given minimal attention. People tend to act independently of each other rather than seek occasions to celebrate together. When rituals are minimized, any excuse to miss them or ignore them is acceptable and expected. (It is true, of course, that rituals might be minimized because they have in fact become meaningless to most participants and ought to be drastically reframed or abandoned.) Sometimes rituals are minimized for other reasons, however. For example, special times in the life of a child might be dismissed because "Daddy has to work today." Or the opportunity to acknowledge an accomplishment might be set aside in favor of phone calls, computer games, or television. Congregational transitions might be discounted with excuses such as "It just takes too much time and everyone is too busy anyway." Or community-wide gatherings and celebrations might be discarded in favor of privatized lives. Minimizing ritual in situations such as these is sometimes a way to escape a painful past or to avoid intimacy and deeper relationships with others.

Some of the following questions might help you explore whether minimized rituals are a problem:

- When rituals are suggested or begun in family or group settings, do you notice a tendency for participants to discount the importance of these celebrations, to avoid participating, or to give the ritual only their halfhearted attention? If so, have you discussed whether this minimizing occurs because people do not find the rituals meaningful or because the rituals need to be reframed to better meet everyone's needs?
- Does your family, friendship group, congregation, or neighborhood have few, if any, real celebrations that bring people together? Are occasions that used to be seen as special avoided now? Has this change taken place since some major loss or trauma in the group?

Imbalanced Rituals

It is important to seek balance when ritualizing special occasions and transitions in our lives, and giving equal attention to everything is, of course, an impossible challenge. Yet we need to be alert to a lack of balance when it occurs. For example, some families tend to adopt the rituals from one side of the family but not the other. Or we engage in rituals for the children in the family but tend to ignore special events and transitions of the parents or grandparents, or vice versa. In congregational life, certain groups within the church might be acknowledged, but others are typically ignored. Or congregations focus most of their ritualizing on the liturgical life of the church but ignore transitions. We might also develop rituals that tend to reflect only the style of the clergy leader or a certain age group or theological viewpoint in the church. In community life, we might find we draw together to deal with natural disasters or violent deaths but never to celebrate new neighborhood initiatives or the accomplishment of community goals. It is also easy to practice imbalanced community rituals by assuming that only Christians are participating and using symbols and language that exclude other religious perspectives.

Recall family, congregational, and community rituals during the past year. In order to gauge whether or not they are relatively well balanced, ask yourself these questions:

- Did our family or our group adopt the rituals of just one side of the family or one part of the group, or did we incorporate the traditions and views of many when we created the rituals?
- Do we tend to celebrate certain kinds of transitions and avoid acknowledging others?
- Do we typically ritualize endings but ignore the waiting times or new beginnings? Or do we ritualize new beginnings without ever acknowledging the endings and time of confusion that might have preceded these new beginnings?
- Do our rituals include newcomers, strangers, and those of differing religious traditions, beliefs, and customs?

Suggestions for Designing Rituals

For rituals to remain transformational, they need to speak to the realities of our individual and communal lives. It is for this reason that rituals need to be continually evaluated. We want to ensure that they continue to address in some profound way the real life transitions we experience and to give us and others the kind of identity and hope that we need in order to confront a changing world. Rituals need to speak to our deepest sense of self, to our very souls.

Moreover, if rituals are to be meaningful, timing is critical. Often we have plenty of time to plan meaningful rituals. At other times, we need to respond quickly to an unexpected situation. In any case, it is wise to remember that the opportunity to assist people by using ritual to bring about healing, a sense of belonging, and transformation can easily pass us by.

To design rituals for yourself or others that will lead to spiritual transformation, I suggest eleven practical guidelines.[5]

1.   The shape and content of any ritual need to grow out of a dialogue with the person(s) whose life cries out for the ritual. Paying attention to the answers to the following questions can enable planners to develop a ritual that will be appropriate. Is the expressed need about a type of transition that is currently taking place or that is expected to take place? If so, is it about an ending, the neutral zone, or a new beginning? Does this transition call the individual or a group into a deeper relationship with God—one that requires letting go of something in order to take hold of something new?

2.   The context within which the ritual will take place is important. Is this ritual better expressed privately or should it involve others? Is this ritual better experienced in the context of a worship service at church, or should it take place in the presence of a small group of friends who will also participate in some way? The content and subject of the ritual as well the wishes of those for whom the ritual is to be celebrated will likely point to an appropriate context.

3.   Rituals often express the inexplicable and take place within a mythological framework, so the choice of symbols and their mythic grounding needs to be carefully explored. If, for example, the individual

needs to work through emotions such as anger, resentment, or fear, these might be symbolized in a drawing or a written statement, and then that piece of paper could be burned as an offering to God. Or the symbol might be placed in a wrapped box and kept in the place where it is frequently seen but not easily reached. In any case, the mythic framework of the ritual probably will include readings from Scripture or other sacred texts and prayer.

The strongest rituals will integrate the three stories mentioned in chapter 1—My Story, Our Story, and God's Story. Each level of ritual helps us express the mysterious side of life and to acknowledge what we cannot fully explain or understand. If we are to express the totality of who we are, we must address all three aspects of Story in our lives.

4. A story lies behind each person's need for ritual. We should allow sufficient time for storytelling. Sometimes, in fact, the core of a ritual is the story about what has taken place but never been entirely shared before. When a person is allowed to tell his or her story and others really listening to that story, great healing can result for both the story-teller and other participants.

5. Some caution needs to be observed when involving others in a ritual. They may be experiencing unresolved grief or issues that are similar to those being ritualized, and some thought should be given to how might be helped to express their feelings during the ritual. Some of those invited to be part of the ritual might be members of other faith traditions, so planners need to be sensitive about which scripture passages, prayers, and symbols are used.

6. Try to keep rituals relatively simple. What they express often escapes words or logic. Let the symbolism of the ritual speak for itself. Meaning might actually be lost in an overly complex ritual. When too many symbols are used, those participating might become confused about what all the symbols mean.

7. Bring the ritual to a definite conclusion. Participants should understand when the ritual is complete and they are free to leave.

8. Allow participants to be creative. Do not be afraid to take a few risks. Many times I have nearly talked myself out of suggesting a

particular ritual because I thought it was too risky or presumptuous of me, only to receive later a deep measure of appreciation for having made the suggestion.

9.   Try to involve as many of your senses as possible. Ask yourself how you might involve taste, smell, hearing, touch, and seeing. Try to engage at least three of the five senses in a ritual.

10. If this ritual is a personal one, do not be afraid to ask those whom you have invited to share in the ritual to provide what you need most at that time. Be in touch with your deepest emotions and needs, and find ways that your friends and family members can respond to contribute toward your healing and wholeness.

11. Be alert for circumstances that seem to cry out for ritualizing. I find I have too often left situations wondering whether I should have suggested engaging in a ritual. Rituals in these situations might have enriched the lives of all those present. Such ritualizing could have deepened our faith and helped all of us experience the relevance of faith to daily life.

Checklists for Designing or Evaluating Rituals

It can be helpful for those who design, or evaluate, rituals for themselves or for larger groups in the church or community to have a checklist to assist in the planning and evaluation process. Below are some questions for different ritualizing contexts that you may find helpful.

Individual Rituals

- Does the ritual you are observing give you a sense of identity that you value or move you toward that sense of identity?
- Does the ritual keep you connected with your higher self? Does it draw out the best in you?
- Do the rituals you observe continue to give you the courage to confront your demons or your fears?

- Are your rituals preparing you for the inevitable major transitions in life?

Family Rituals

- Do your family rituals fit everyone's daily schedule? If not, how can you negotiate a better time for all?
- Do your family rituals draw you closer together as a family and give everyone a sense of family identity and belonging?
- Do your family rituals affirm the value of all members of the family, young and old, male and female?
- Do your family rituals anticipate the transitions of family members? Are all birthdays observed in some way? Are children's transitions acknowledged and celebrated as they grow up? Are adults' or teens' new work positions or achievements noted? Are accomplishments and transitions of elderly members of the family acknowledged?
- Do your family rituals prepare your family for deep changes and crises, such as serious illness or death? Are there rituals to help caregivers as well as those who experience the significant transition, the ill, and the dying?

Congregational Rituals

- Are congregational rituals still meaningful even as times change, or have they over the years become largely ceremonial and lost their meaning, purpose, and capacity to transform?
- Are the rituals of the congregation creative and imaginative or have they become overly routine and boring?
- Do congregational rituals affirm the value of all in the congregation, young and old, male and female, the charter member and the newcomer or the stranger, those who give much time to the congregation and those who minister largely outside it?
- Do congregational rituals affirm the congregation's past, present, and future in some way?
- Are congregational rituals relevant to the times in which we live?

That is, do they observe the significant transitions taking place in members' lives and in the communal life of the congregation itself?
- Do congregational rituals speak to the depth of transitions that occur?

Community Rituals

Community-wide rituals are the most challenging of ritual observances, because these rituals need to address people across a wide spectrum of religious beliefs and cultural mores. Planners must find symbols that will not exclude some people or offend others. These ritual must be timely and address issues thought to be important by a large number of people within the community.

- Do the rituals in which the community engages address a transition or crisis that needs to be placed within a broader context?
- Are the symbols that will be used broad enough to include everyone who chooses to participate, whether they are Christian, Jewish, Moslem, Hindu, Buddhist, or atheist; rich or poor; well known or strangers; practitioners of ethnic traditions common or unusual in the community? Will all likely be able to enter wholly into the ritual?
- Are the right people present? Should this ritual include civic leaders, the superintendent of schools, the police chief or sheriff, religious or ethnic leaders, or other public figures from the community?
- What is the best place to hold the ritual? How much space is needed? Does the ritual need to be held on a specific site, for example, to redeem a given space from violence or to acknowledge a specific loss?

Mutual Accountability for Ritualizing

As individuals and congregations move toward strengthening their ritual practices, people might find it helpful to work with others and covenant in some way to be mutually accountable for the ritual. There are any number of ways this might be done. For example, individuals who wish to strengthen their spiritual lives and wring more meaning out of the transitions in life might simply invite another person or several people to help hold them accountable for what it is they say they wish to do and how they want to grow. Several people on a similar journey might covenant to meet with one another, or an individual might make a commitment to another person or group to meet with a spiritual director or guide, their clergyperson, a small faith community or prayer or study group, or other friends. The one making the covenant might promise to check in with the partners at specific intervals and give them permission to ask questions about how the new ritual is going. Whether between friends or in groups, mutual accountability—each person holding the other accountable—is always more respectful than unilateral a process.

Even in a relationship with a spiritual director or pastor, individuals might expect accountability to be practiced in a spirit of mutuality. Those covenanting, for example, will want to be treated as adults rather like children who are being checked on by a superior. They will want opportunities to discuss ways they are growing and to ask for suggestions, resources, or feedback—whatever is needed, when it is needed. As much as possible, those seeking spiritual guidance should take the initiative and be able to change the contract as their own needs change. They can expect that their own individual styles and tastes in ritualizing will be treated with great respect and that the mentor will not impose his or her own preferences on them. They should insist on never being shamed for their shortcomings or failure to ritualize perfectly.

A great time for families to talk about their commitments to family ritualizing might be during a family meeting or perhaps at a monthly supper or at the conclusion of one of their regular times for ritual together. The above guidelines for mutuality would apply. Everyone in the family should have a say in designing and evaluating the rituals. Feelings should be openly expressed in a mutually respectful manner, and allowance for differences should always be made.

Ritual planning groups in congregations also need some mutual accountability. For example, if ritual becomes part of a group's regular gatherings, then all should have a voice in evaluating the rituals periodically, sharing ideas for rituals, and helping to lead ritual if they so desire and have the gifts to do so. Some groups in the church might have more responsibility for congregational rituals, and they will have a special responsibility to take seriously the types of evaluation

questions and checklists suggested here as well as to seek community
input and feedback and to continue learning about the role and design
of ritual.

In the larger community, evaluation of ritual should include a wide
variety of community constituents in order to ensure that the rituals are
inclusive and that people from non-Christian traditions are included in
planning, leadership, and evaluation, so that ritualizing occasions bring
the community closer together rather than reenforcing estrangement and
prejudices. Respect for diversity will need to be high on any evaluation
checklist in these situations.

Reflection Exercises

1. Recall a recent ritual conducted in a family, congregational, or com-
    munity setting and with several other people apply the eleven sugges-
    tions listed on pages 106-108. Discover how the ritual fared when
    measured by these criteria.

2. Take a piece of paper and divide it into quadrants. (Or with a group
    of people, do the same on a large piece of newsprint.) Label one
    quadrant "obligatory," another "rigid," a third "minimizing," and
    the fourth "unbalanced." Leave a large square in the middle of the
    paper marked "healthy, transformative rituals." Then with your
    family or a church committee or group of friends, note where you
    would place various rituals you have experienced during the past
    couple of years. Note whether any pattern emerges. Respectfully
    discuss any differences of opinion among members of the group.
    Explore how one person might see as obligatory a ritual another
    finds freeing, for example, or how one thinks a ritual is minimiz-
    ing and another thinks it simply needs to be reframed because it is
    outdated. Note where you agree. Discover how you might work
    together both when you agree and when you disagree about some
    facet of ritualizing.

3. Invite each person in a group from an extended family, a congre-
    gation, or a community to recall a time when he or she felt like the
    newcomer, outsider, or stranger when a ritual was underway. Ask each

person to share the emotions they remember feeling in that situation. Brainstorm together what would have increased your sense of belonging and being respected in such situations.

4. In your journal, reflect on times when your personal ritualizing has been most transformative as well as times when your personal rituals might have had some destructive tendencies. Think of ways that you might covenant with a friend, spiritual mentor, or small group to continue to use ritual in your life in healthy ways that lead to spiritual transformation and assist you through the ongoing transitions in your life.

5. Invite several non-Christian leaders to one of your congregational meetings and talk together about how you might work together to design a community ritual that would be inclusive of all.

CHAPTER 7

Planning for a Ministry of Ritual

We have presented several dozen rituals throughout this book for use by individuals, families, congregations, and the public. Some rituals are daily practices that help keep us in spiritual shape and in a growing relationship with ourselves, those around us, and God. These regular rituals also help us to prepare for the difficult transitions in our lives. Other rituals provided in this book are specifically designed for such times of change. Some focus on endings, the first step of all transitions. Others provide a way to symbolize and honor the uncomfortable neutral zone with its characteristic confusion, frustration, and waiting. And others provide a way to celebrate new beginnings. Some rituals incorporate all stages of the transition process.

We as a people find ourselves living in a world of rapid and systemic change in every arena of life. Although such change often taxes our capacity to cope and presents us with tremendous challenges as a human community, it is the reality of this time in history. It also provides an exceptional opportunity for communities of faith to minister in the world with some unique resources, albeit often latent resources: our ability to ritualize. The church has not used this gift as fully and creatively as it might. By focusing most of our ritual around Sunday worship and the celebration of specific sacraments, we have neglected to extend the ministry of ritual into the Monday-through-Saturday lives of our members and to offer it as a resource for transforming the people in our communities. The gifts needed to carry out a substantial ministry of ritual are present in our religious traditions and in our people. We just have not opened these gifts and applied them broadly. We have not mined the possibilities, the ways ritual can lead us through change to produce less brokenness and more spiritual transformation and zest for life.

Ritual can be a powerful way to help us let go of our attachment to the way life has been and to face our fear of loss and grief. In the neutral zone of transitions, ritual can help us through the anxiety of waiting, the struggle of dealing with the unknown, and the sometimes confusing discernment about the future. And ritual helps us recognize when we have come to the point of new beginnings and to celebrate this new adventure. Individuals, families, congregations, and society as a whole experience these processes of letting go, working through, and beginning again. Denying and avoiding transitions simply do not work, and merely talking does not seem to have the same transformative effect as combining conversation and words with symbol and gesture in ritual.

Clearly readers of this book are encouraged to use any rituals that fit a specific situation and your own need and preferences. In this way, the book can be an ongoing personal resource for you. However, if the church is to draw on what is potentially one of its greatest gifts to the world, then congregations must develop a systemic strategy for providing a ministry of ritual. This requires discernment, planning, and organization. Most of all, it involves catching a new vision of ministry as we enter the next millennium. For those who are excited about their congregation developing such a ministry, the question is, How to we get from where we are today to offering a full-fledged ministry of ritual to our members and the larger community?

Initiating a Ministry of Ritual

Among the first issues to consider is who might initiate such a ministry effort and under what circumstances. Clearly, interest and support on the part of the pastor and the staff will be essential; frequently they will be the initiators of these efforts as well. A pastor or church administrator might bring this book to the church staff to study, so they can begin to implement some of these ideas. Once the staff begins to understand the value of ritual for their personal lives, staff relationships, and their work, then they might approach the church board about a ministry of ritual. Or staff members might talk about ritual with people involved in the ministry programs for which they are resource people and liaisons.

(Chapter 2 presents numerous ideas about how ritualizing might be built into the various ministry programs of the congregation.)

If all the staff and many key lay leaders receive at least some initial training or exposure to ritual, they can be on the lookout for opportunities to ritualize transitions in the ministry of the congregation and will be more likely to support such an effort. Then, for example, when the congregation is about to enter into a new strategic planning effort or any other major initiative that members will easily recognize as the beginning of change, congregation leaders will be in a position to take advantage of these excellent opportunities to introduce ritualizing as part of acknowledging congregational transitions.

Because of the nature of their work and because they serve people of all ages within the congregation, leaders of Christian education and worship ministries can be of great help when designing ways to educate congregational members about the powerful role of ritual in helping us turn transitions into real opportunities for spiritual transformation. Certain seasons of the church year might provide easy opportunities for introducing such material. For example, Advent and Lent— seasons when we often think about change in our lives—are traditionally times when congregations hold special adult education series or family-oriented events.

Another especially ripe opportunity for introducing members to the role of ritual is during crisis and loss. Both staff and lay ministers who work in the ministry of pastoral care would, therefore, be key players in a ministry of ritual. Many of these pastoral care ministers, however, will benefit from an opportunity to study the stages of transitions as well as ways to ritualize endings, the neutral zone, and new beginnings.

The social outreach committees of congregations as well as the congregation's clergy are likely to be the key people to reach out to other congregations and community groups to discover meaningful opportunities for a ministry of ritual in the larger community. In this arena, as within the congregation itself, work will usually need to be done collaboratively. Sensitivity to the variety of traditions and belief systems, ethnic customs, and the value of working as partners will all be critical in this effort.

The opportunities and potential entry points for initiating such a ministry of ritual are numerous. Any leader or member might initiate such an idea in the congregation. The most successful strategies will involve several leaders, opportunities to study and to try out transitional rituals, and a process for evaluating and learning from these early experiences.

New Directions Church, Centerville, U.S.A.

The 300-member New Directions Church is located in a town of 3,000 people. Some of its members own businesses and farms in the community. Many others work in one of the local manufacturing plants in the county, teach in area schools, or are retired. Jerry Johnsen, pastor of New Directions Church, read *Transforming Rituals* several months ago. He was excited about the ideas the book presented but wondered how to start such a process in his congregation. So he decided to take his interest to his clergy colleagues in the local ministerial when the group next met. As they talked about the amount of change church members and the community as a whole were experiencing, the conversation grew animated. In fact, the subject was put on the agenda of several more of their meetings. As a result of those conversations, the clergy began to identify several community issues or transitions that occur every year as well as to anticipate a plant closing that was to happen in a few months. They decided they needed to be more active in assisting the community through those transitions.

During the next several months, several of the clergy took their concerns back to their own congregations. They also began to reach out to leaders in the Hmong community and to Native American leaders on a reservation that bordered the town. Together representatives of these three groups planned and provided leadership for several ritual celebrations in the town over the next several months. They were joined by a number of interested lay leaders from each of their respective congregations or groups.

Meanwhile, Pastor Jerry had introduced *Transforming Rituals* to both the church board and the newly formed strategic planning committee at New Directions Church. All these leaders read the book, and an evening was set aside to discuss it. The leaders decided to initiate the strategic planning process in their congregation by using the Ritual for Strategic Planning. They also continued prayer and discernment about whether their congregation might be called to a ministry of ritual beyond anything they had done before. When the strategic planning process was completed several months later, one of the major goals was to initiate a ministry of ritual. Here is that section of their plan:

Ministry of Ritual

Plan for the New Directions Church

Vision Statement

New Directions Church will be a congregation that builds an awareness of the transformative power of ritual among its members and the larger community, especially during times of transition. A variety of experiences and resources will be offered to assist members to design, participate in, and evaluate rituals for transitional times in their own lives, their neighborhoods, and in the life of the congregation.

Due Date	Objectives
May 2000	*Objective A*: Use church print media, bulletin boards, and sermons and announcements to begin to raise awareness of the role of ritual in our everyday lives and its potential transformative power during times of transition.
September 2000	*Objective B*: Engage the entire staff of the church in a collaborative effort to learn more about transitional processes in the lives of individuals, families, the congregation, and the larger community and potential transformation role of ritual during these times. Have the staff begin to use ritual in their own meetings and ministry together as a way to model for the rest of the congregation.
October 2000	*Objective C*: Design a simple booklet of opening and closing rituals for committees and established groups, and train group leaders in these processes.
November 2000	*Objective D*: Sponsor a three-session adult forum series to focus on each of the three contexts for ritualizing transitions: individual/family, congregation, and the larger community.

Februrary 2001	*Objective E*: Encourage two or three established small groups in the church (such as a women's circle, a faith sharing group, or a parenting group) to study the book *Transforming Rituals*.
May 2001	*Objective F*: Celebrate ritually at least one ending, one neutral time, and one new beginning in congregation life during the year.
June 2001	*Objective G*: Collaborate with the local ministerial group and the Hmong and Native American communities to ritualize three annual events or transitions in the town and the ending, neutral time, and new beginning related to the closing of the manufacturing plant.

New Hope Valley Church, Coastal, U.S.A.

Located in a middle-class first-ring suburb of a large metropolitan area, New Hope Valley Church is a forward-looking congregation of 2,000 households. Many young families as well as empty nesters and retired people belong to the church. About 10 percent of the adults in the congregation participate in small faith sharing groups that meet monthly. The leadership team for the small group ministry learned about *Transforming Rituals* at a conference they all attended and returned to New Hope Valley excited about introducing the materials as their theme for the coming year. For several months, the small groups read chapters of the book, discussed the study questions, shared their experiences with transitions and ritual practices in their own lives, and began to incorporate ritual into their regular monthly gatherings.

Within two months, several people were so excited about the possibilities they were discussing that they requested a meeting with the pastor and president of the church board to share their enthusiasm. Subsequently, they were asked to make a presentation to the entire staff and board. Soon a ministry of ritual task force was formed and asked to make recommendations to the board for establishing a new ministry and implementing it over a three-year period. The task force carefully studied not only *Transforming Rituals* but several other resources on ritual, talked with members of the small group about their experiences using the ritual materials, and surveyed the staff and lay ministry leaders about how rituals were now used in the church and community and how their congregation was helping people deal with transitions. Six months later, they recommended the following three-year plan to the church board of New Hope Valley Church.

Strategic Plan

Ritual Ministry in New Hope Valley Church

Vision Statement

New Hope Valley Church ministers in a rapidly changing world. It engages in ritualizing ministry at the critical transition junctures—endings, neutral times, and new beginnings—in the congregation and in the lives of its members and people in the broader community. Through teaching/coaching, encouraging/supporting, modeling, advocating, and evaluating, it prepares people to design, lead, and evaluate rituals in various life arenas and transitions.

Year 1

Objective A: Recruit, train, and support leaders for a ministry of ritualizing transitions.

Action Steps

1. Interested staff and members provide a short in-service for all church leaders about ritual and transitions.
2. Staff members explore their roles in teaching/coaching, encouraging/supporting, modeling, advocating, and evaluating rituals for transitions. Personnel committee integrates these roles into expectations for staff performance. Staff begins to use ritual in its meetings.
3. Staff and members identify and recruit a core group of interested and appropriately gifted lay people to serve on a ritual ministry task force. They study the book *Transforming Rituals* as a foundational training text for their work and use rituals together as their own work develops.

Objective B: Use a variety of methods to raise members' awareness about the role of ritual and its potential transformative power during transitions in individual and communal life.

Action Steps

1. The ritual ministry task force and congregation staff members use church print media, bulletin boards, sermon illustrations, and weekly announcements to relate that week's liturgy to possible ritual practices in the home and community.
2. The ritual ministry task force designs a simple booklet of opening and closing rituals for church committees and established groups and train group leaders in these processes.
3. The ritual ministry task force sponsors a three-session adult forum series to focus on each of the three contexts for ritualizing transitions: individual/family, congregation, and the larger community.
4. At least three additional established small groups in the church (such as a women's circle, young adult group, and the parenting group) study the book *Transforming Rituals*.

Objective C: The congregation celebrates ritually at least one ending, one neutral time, and one new beginning in the life of the congregation during the year.

Objective D: The ritual ministry task force designs and coordinates an evaluation process to assess progress on introducing a ministry of ritual to the congregation.

Year 2

Objective E: Provide several new opportunities for members to learn about the role of ritual during time of transitions.

Action Steps

1. Additional established groups in the church study the book *Transforming Rituals* and other suggested resources on ritualizing in

daily life. (Groups might include specially formed study groups, youth groups, and couple's groups.)

2. Several ministry committees with potential roles in ritualizing (such as Christian education, worship, pastoral care, youth ministry, evangelism, and social outreach committees) study *Transforming Rituals* as their in-service learning for the year.

3. The ritual ministry task force prepares a special booklet and other resources for ritualizing within families to be given to parents and introduced during baptismal preparation/child dedication classes and when children register for the church school. Other age-appropriate resources are introduced in the confirmation class.

Objective F: Each major program area of the congregation develops and implements at least one new way to integrate ritualizing of transitions into their area of ministry. These rituals might include ideas from chapters 2-5 of *Transforming Rituals*.

Objective G: The congregational governing board incorporates ritual into the annual congregational meeting and develops rituals for initiating a new ministry, terminating a ministry, or celebrating ministry in progress.

Objective H: The social outreach committee (or other appropriate committee) in collaboration with the ritual ministry task force and the church staff explore possibilities for public ritual with other neighboring congregations (including those of non-Christian traditions).

Objective I: The ritual ministry task force designs and coordinates a process for evaluating the congregation's work on ritualizing transitions.

Year 3

Objective J: Working collaboratively with other neighborhood congregations, the ritual ministry task force and groups responsible for several major ministry areas of the congregation provide a community-wide workshop or retreat on the relationship among life transitions, ritual, and spiritual transformation.

Objective K: The ritual ministry task force and other designated ministry teams in the congregation initiate coalitions and networks with neighborhood congregations and groups to address issues of transition in the community and how to offer resources on ritual.

Action Steps

1. The ritual ministry task force in collaboration with the social outreach committee organizes training for a team of core lay leaders to prepare them to work with other congregations and religious traditions to design, organize, and lead rituals in the public arena around transitional issues.
2. The core leader team works with leaders of other congregations and groups to design and coordinate at least three public rituals that acknowledge community transitions.
3. Leaders from each of the represented community congregations and groups seek public feedback from participants in these rituals and meet to evaluate these ritualizing experiences, assess future needs, and plan for additional community involvement.

Conclusion

In today's society, people encounter transition in every arena of life—family, friendship, work, political life, neighborhood, and church. We are all experiencing rapid, cumulative change. Often people and institutions do not know where to turn to find meaning in the midst of change and to secure resources to see them through what feels overwhelming. People are crying out for hope and meaning, however. They yearn for something that ties together their often segmented lives in a way that gives new meaning and joy.

This book provides some approaches that draw on the deepest traditions and resources of our churches to address these very human issues in our time. It seeks to provide ritual processes that help to integrate the stages of transition—endings, the neutral zones, and new beginnings—and to do so in a way that also integrates arenas of our life that often seem disconnected from one another. People need to integrate all these aspects of life in order to feel whole, to find meaning, and to be transformed, particularly in a time in history that is itself marked by great transformation and change.

I urge you to talk with your friends about the transitions you encounter, the practices of ritual you use or do not use, how your congregation ritualizes its own transitions, and the role you might play together in the public arena. Share your ideas; try out some of the rituals in this book. Create you own new rituals. Evaluate them and incorporate those learnings into your next efforts. Learn from your friends and family members. This book only touches the surface of what is possible. There are as many ideas for creative and meaningful rituals that can transform lives as there are people who will engage in them. Ritualizing transitions is an important ministry of any congregation as we enter into a new era in the church. All of us can be part of this important ministry of creativity and healing.

Reflection Exercises

1. Discuss with others in your congregation what your church does now to encourage ritual for individuals and families, for congregational transitions, and in the larger public arena.

2. At a family meeting, brainstorm some rituals you would like to covenant to do together in the next several months.

3. List several people in your congregation with whom you might talk about the ideas in this book. How can you be an initiator of a ministry of ritual in your own congregation? Which decision makers and groups might be most receptive to such a ministry?

4. In quiet time alone or with a small group, develop an image for a ministry of ritual for your congregation. What image would capture the notions of integrating personal, congregational, and community life and the three stages of transition? What symbol would speak to the resulting spiritual transformation? Include your image as part of your prayer life for several days, and see how it informs your own discernment process.

5. If you see a spiritual director, guide, or mentor, discuss your own transitions and practices of ritual with that person. Enter a process of discernment and then covenant to use ritual in your own spiritual life.

6. If you are a staff member or lay leader in your own congregation and are enthusiastic about the possibilities for a ministry of ritual, list three steps you might take in the next two months to encourage your congregation toward this sort of ministry. Then pray for guidance and proceed!

APPENDIX A

Remembrance and Commendation
of a Stillborn Child or for Use after a Miscarriage

1. This service may be used as a simple prayer service, as a memorial service, or as a funeral service (if the remains are to be present).
2. Some families will want nothing more than prayers at the hospital. Others will find the presence of family, friends, and members of the congregation to be a source of great comfort in their time of loss. Parents should be invited to choose what would be most helpful to them, including where the service will be held—in the hospital, at home, or in the church.

PRAYER OF CONSOLATION
3. A prayer of consolation is offered.

PSALM LITANY
4. Psalm 139:1-15 is read, using verse 23 as an antiphon at the beginning and after verses 6,12, and 15.

Leader: Search me out, O God, and know my heart; try me and know my restless thoughts.

Congregation: Search me out, O God, and know my heart; try me and know my restless thoughts.

L: Lord, you have searched me out and known me;
you know my sitting down and my rising up;
you discern my thoughts from afar.
You trace my journeys and my resting-places

and are acquainted with all my ways.
Indeed, there is not a word on my lips,
but you, O Lord, know it altogether.
You press upon me behind and before
and lay your hand upon me.
Such knowledge is too wonderful for me;
it is so high that I cannot attain to it.
Where can I go then from your Spirit?
Where can I flee from your presence?

C: Search me out, O God, and know my heart; try me and know my restless thoughts.

L: If I climb up to heaven, you are there;
if I make the grave my bed, you are there also.
If I take the wings of the morning and dwell
in the uttermost parts of the sea,
even there your hand will lead me
and your right hand hold me fast.
If I say, "Surely the darkness will cover me,
and the light around me turn to night,"
darkness is not dark to you;
the night is as bright as the day;
darkness and light to you are both alike.
For you yourself created my inmost parts;
you knit me together in my mother's womb.

C: Search me out, O God, and know my heart; try me and know my restless thoughts.

L: I will thank you because I am marvelously made;
your works are wonderful, and I know it well.
My body was not hidden from you,
while I was being made in secret
and woven in the depths of the earth.
Your eyes beheld my limbs, yet unfinished in the womb;
all of them were written in your book;
they were fashioned day by day,
when as yet there was none of them.

C: Search me out, O God, and know my heart; try me and know my restless thoughts.

WORDS OF COMFORT
5. The following or other appropriate words are offered.

P: The Lord spoke through the prophet Isaiah saying, "For behold, I am about to create new heavens and a new earth; the former things shall not be remembered or come into mind. But be glad and rejoice for ever in what I am creating; for I am about to create Jerusalem as a joy, and its people as a delight. No more shall there be in it an infant that lives but a few days" (65:17-18, 20a). In that day when God creates the new heavens and a new earth, we will not need to gather to mourn the loss of a child. But on this day, we come with sadness to seek the comfort of God. We mourn the loss of a child known to the mother who carried it, to the father who generated it, and to us in hopes and dreams.

C: O Holy Spirit, Comforter, be present with us.

6. The Prayer of the Day may be said.
7. A hymn may be sung.

NAMING THE CHILD
8. The parents may publicly name their child.

P: The word of the Lord came to Jeremiah saying, "Before I formed you in the womb I knew you...." And the name "Jesus" was given to God's only child to be a sign of salvation and the means by which we may know and remember God's lovingkindness and mercy. We name this child today, so that we may remember her/his coming among us, and we ask God to bless our remembering.
(To the parents): What will you name this child?

Parents: We name her/him _____. *(The parents may also mention the significance of the chosen name.)*

P: O child whom we have barely known, we call you ____(name)____. Receive this name as a sign of your uniqueness to us and before God. By this name you will be remembered.

9. One or more lessons and/or psalms are read.

10. A sermon or meditation may be preached.

11. A hymn may be sung.

12. The Apostles' Creed may be said.

13. Prayers are said in thanksgiving for God's love for the child, and for the parents and all who mourn.

14. When Holy Communion is celebrated, the service continues with sharing the peace. The commendation then follows the post-communion canticle and prayer. When there is no Communion, the service continues with the Lord's Prayer.

BLESSING AND COMMENDATION

15. This blessing and commendation may be offered.

P: O Child __(or, name)__ , we entrust you to God who created you. May you return to the One who formed us out of the dust of the earth.

C: Amen

P: Merciful Creator, your Holy Spirit intercedes for us even when we do not know how to pray. Send your Spirit now to comfort us in these days of need and loss, and help us to commend __(name/"this child"/ "this pregnancy")__ to your merciful care; through Jesus Christ our Savior.

C: Amen

P: May this child __(or, name)__ and all the departed, through the mercy of God, rest in peace.

C: Amen

P: Let us go forth in peace.

C: In the name of Christ. Amen

SUGGESTED LESSON AND HYMNS

Traditional funeral lessons, psalms, and hymns fit this service. In addition, the following may be especially appropriate:

Deuteronomy 33:27a	*There's A Wideness in God's Mercy*
Isaiah 40:27-31	*My Hope Is Built on Nothing Less*
Jeremiah 31:15	*O God, Our Help in Ages Past*
Romans 8:26-27	*Jesus, Savior, Pilot Me*
1 John 3:1-2	*When Peace, Like a River, Attendeth My Way*
Luke 18:15-17	*Children of the Heavenly Father*
	There Is a Balm in Gilead
	Give Me Jesus (Traditional)
	Precious Lord, Take my Hand

APPENDIX B

Planning a Blessing/Ritual after Divorce

Identify some important elements:

1. Where will it be? At home, in a church or chapel, at a favorite place or outdoor spot, and so forth?
2. Who will be there? Only you, friends, family, children, neighbors, ex-spouse, and so forth?
3. What items might you use? Symbolic and re-collective things such as a wedding ring, pictures, flowers, wedding dress, items of meaning to you as a couple, and so forth?
4. What songs/music could you use?
5. What stories might be a part of this ceremony? What actions?
6. What outcome are you looking for?

Elements of a prayer/statement that could be read:

1. Acknowledge the pain and hurt of the broken relationship.
2. Express a desire to leave the old behind and live the life this change brings you.
3. Acknowledge the support and source of your strength (family friends, faith, counselor, support group, and so forth.)
4. Express the feelings you have about stepping into a new life and request the qualities that it takes to continue your life of spiritual growth.

Reprinted with permission of Adaire Lassonde, SSND, LISW, Office for Separated and Divorced, Catholic Charities, Archdiocese of St. Paul and Minneapolis.

APPENDIX C

Prayer Vigil Network Liturgy for Victims of Violence

By gathering for a brief prayer vigil we will stand in solidarity with our brothers and sisters against that which destroys our city by destroying its citizens. Whenever someone is killed, we are all affected.

CALL TO PRAYER

SCRIPTURE READINGS *(in unison)*
Romans 12:14-21
Psalm 23
[The text for these readings was provided to participants.]

PRAYERS OF THE COMMUNITY GATHERED
Anyone is invited to offer prayer. Please close your prayer by saying, "Lord, in your mercy." Everyone may then respond by saying, "Hear our prayer."

THE LORD'S PRAYER *(joining hands)*

HYMN
"We shall live in peace ... someday"
"We shall live in hope ... today"

SCRIPTURE READING *(in unison)*
During this reading, the ground will be anointed with oil as a sign of healing and hope for our city and all of its citizens.
Matthew 5:43-48
[The text for these readings was provided to participants.]

Closing Prayer

Reprinted from the liturgy held on July 10, 1999, for the 69th victim of violence in Indianapolis, Indiana, in 1999. The liturgy was prepared by The Church Federation of Greater Indianapolis, 1100 West 42nd Street, Suite 345, Indianapolis, IN 46208; 317-926-5371.

APPENDIX D

A Ritual to Honor the Movement into Puberty

GATHERING

(Gather around the central table. Arranged on the table is a large bowl of water, a tea kettle, and space for candles and tokens.)
Leader: I invite each of you to remember a woman who inspired you.
(Each speaks in turn, lighting a candle and pouring herself a cup of raspberry leaf tea.)

INVOCATION

L: Today we gather in the names of these women who have helped us in our life's journey. We thank God for the blessings they have given to us, and ask God's presence here, especially the fierce and gentle mothering energy of God. We remember especially El Shaddai, the great breasted one, who provides for her children's needs, from Abraham and Sarah even to this day. May she bless our work today.

STORIES

The First Lesson
(Each tells a story of the movement from chaos to order from her adolescence. All toast each story with tea.)

The Second Lesson
Genesis 1:26-31

The Third Lesson
John 3:1-7, 16

Bringing the Gifts

L: We offer our wisdom to you, Cara. Because you are already wise, take our stories and our wishes into your own soul as our offerings to you. Choose what will comfort and inspire you, and let the rest be a sign of our affection for you.
(The altar is prepared. As each offers her wisdom, her token is place[d] on the central table.)

BLESSING

(As each offers her verbal blessing, she drops a flower petal in the bowl of water. Then all gather around Cara and lay hands on her.)
All: Cara, we will be here for you in the coming months and years. We are pleased to welcome you into the company of women. We are a sacred company, blessed by the Holy One for our work of nurturing life. You walk with us now.
L: You have been baptized by the Holy Spirit, and created by a loving God. Nothing can separate you from the power of your creator to bring you into life.
All: Amen

SENDING

L: God give birth to each of you in the days and years to come. May you be blessed by clarity of purpose and steadfast confidence in God's love for you. Amen

A Ritual to Honor the Movement into Puberty

GATHERING

(Gather around the fire.)
L: I invite each of you to remember a woman who inspired you with her love and courage. In doing so, we gather the memories and spirits of women who have made us who we are.
(Each speaks in turn, lighting her candle as she speaks.)

INVOCATION

L: Today we gather in the names of these women who have helped us in our life's journey. We thank God for the blessings they have given to us and ask God's presence here, especially the fierce and gentle mothering energy of God. We remember especially El Shaddai, the great breasted one, who provides for her children's needs, from Abraham and Sarah even to this day. May she bless our work this evening.
(Regather in the house, arranging the candles on the central table around the basin.)
L: Our ancient brothers remembered the stories of inspiring women—women of wisdom, courage, and great love.
(Tell the story of Abigail, 1 Samuel 25:14-42.)

STORIES

The First Lessons
L: We each have our own stories of wisdom, courage, and great love, all traits that can carry us through times of change and becoming.

(Each tells a story of a time from her own adolescence when fear became courage and she came to know love instead of fear.)

The Second Lesson
Isaiah 43:1-7

The Third Lesson
Luke 1:46-50

THE BLESSINGS

L: We offer our blessings to you, Abbie. Because you are already wise, take our stories and our wishes into your own soul as our offerings to you. Choose what will comfort and inspire you, and let the rest be a sign of our affection for you.
(As each offers her blessing, she places a token of it on the central table. When all have spoken, we gather around Abbie and lay hands on her.)
All: Abbie, we will be here for you in the coming months and years. We are pleased to welcome you into the company of women. We are a sacred company, blessed by the Holy One for our work of nurturing life. You walk with us now.
L: You have been baptized by the Holy Spirit, and created by a loving God. Nothing can separate you from the power of your creator to bring you into life.
All: Amen

THANKSGIVING

L: Abbie, you have already been a blessing to us. We look forward to your growing.
(Each offers one way Abbie has been a blessing already, toasting with raspberry leaf tea.)

SENDING

L: God give birth to each of you in the days and years to come. May you be blessed by clarity of purpose and steadfast confidence in God's love for you. Go with courage and peace. Amen

Reprinted with the permission of Catherine Malotky, who prepared these rituals for her daughters.

A Service of the Blessing of the Animals

COLLECT

Most High, Omnipotent, Good Lord, grant Your people grace to renounce gladly the vanities of this world; that following the way of blessed Francis, we may for love of You delight Your whole creation with perfectness of joy through Jesus Christ our Lord, Who lives and reigns with You and the Holy Spirit, one God, for ever and ever. Amen

HYMN: "All Things Bright and Beautiful"

PSALM 148:7-14

READING: Genesis 1:20-26

HOMILY

HYMN: "Hymn of Promise" by Natalie Sleeth

PRAYER OF THE FAITHFUL

Leader: Almighty God, we praise your name as the Creator of all. We worship you the Creator and ask you to be with us and bless all of your creatures.
Response: Lord, hear our prayer.
Leader: Help us to have fuller insights into the rights and needs of all creatures; we pray to you, O Lord.

Response: Lord, hear our prayer.
Leader: We ask you to comfort all your creatures who are in pain or suffer; we pray to you, O Lord.
Response: Lord, hear our prayer.
Leader: We pray for all animals, birds, and fish whom you created; O Lord.
Response: Lord, hear our prayer.
Leader: We pray that all people will be moved to reach out with respect and love to all of your creation after the example of St. Francis.
Response: Lord, hear our prayer.

ANNOUNCEMENTS

THE BLESSING OF THE ANIMALS

CLOSING PRAYER: "Peace Prayer of St. Francis" (sung)

DISMISSAL

The offering from this service will be give to the Animal Control Charity Fund of Howard County.

Reprinted from "A Service of the Blessing of the Animals," St. John's Episcopal Church, Ellicott City, Maryland, October 4, 1998. Used by permission.

Service of Word and Prayer after School Violence

PRELUDE

"Why"
"The Lord Is My Shepherd"
"The Lord's Prayer

(Please stand.)

CALL TO WORSHIP

P: O Lord, our God,
C: Have mercy on us.
P: Hear our cry and come to our aid,
C: For we are broken and crushed.
P: Why? O Lord, why?
C: Why do our children lie dead?
P: Why do the innocent suffer?
C: Why should our children have to live in fear?
P: Why should we trust anymore?
C: Your people are crying, Lord.
P: Listen to the crying of your children.
C: Hear our cry and come to our aid.

HYMN "God of Grace and God of Glory"

THE GREETING

P: The grace of our Lord Jesus Christ, the love of God, and the communion of the Holy Spirit be with you all.
C: And also with you.

PRAYER FOR THE DAY

P: Let us pray.
C: O God, we are consumed by grief and what we have witnessed in our community. Come to our aid, walk with us, hold us, strengthen us, and give us courage for the days ahead, through Jesus Christ our Lord. Amen

(Please be seated.)

WELCOME

THE FIRST LESSON   Micah 4:1-5
THE SECOND LESSON   Psalm 130

AN OFFERTORY
"My Heart Yearns for Thee"

(Please stand.)

THE GOSPEL LESSON   Matthew 5:1-12

(Please be seated.)

HOMILY

(Please stand.)

HYMN "A Mighty Fortress Is Our God"

THE PRAYERS OF THE FAITHFUL

P: Let us pray for the whole people of God, this community, our nation, and the world who grieve with us.

(Silence for reflection)

P: For the families of those who were slain yesterday. Who waited through the night, whose children and loved ones laid on the cold floor of the school,
C: Hold them in your loving arms.
P: For the wounded and for those who still fight for their lives in hospitals,
C: Hold them in your loving arms.
P: For the families of those children who have killed, wounded, and brought fear to others,
C: Hold them in your loving arms.
P: For the children and school staff who saw sights and heard sounds that will forever scar their souls,
C: Hold them in your loving arms.
P: For the children and staff who sought refuge behind locked doors and who endured an afternoon of terror,
C: Hold them in your loving arms.
P: For families, parents, friends, and loved ones who endured waiting and watching and hope and despair,
C: Hold them in your loving arms.
P: For the police officers, advocates, teachers, pastors, counselors, doctors, nurses, and others who showed bravery, offered care, extended kindness, and endured through the day,
C: Hold them in your loving arms.
P: For all school children and teachers in our community and the world who are shocked and who will live in fear after witnessing what happened here yesterday,
C: Hold them in your loving arms.
P: For this community who is broken, weeping, and whose vision for this community has been shattered,
C: Hold them in your loving arms.
P: For this community who is broken, weeping, and whose vision for this community has been shattered,
C: Hold them in your loving arms.
P: For our church, our nation, and the world who grieve and who long for the end of violence and hatred,
C: Give us wisdom and courage.

P: For us, who are gathered here, that we may not give up on life, this community, our kids, and the vision you have for our world. Give us wisdom and courage to be your church, to be peacemakers, to care for all our children, and to unite with all to make our world safe and secure for all. Lord in your mercy,
C: Hear our prayers.
P: Into your hand O lord, we commend all for whom we pray, trusting in your mercy, through Jesus Christ, your Son, our Lord.
C: Amen

(Please be seated.)

HYMN "Abide With Me"

THE LORD'S PRAYER

BENEDICTION

P: The Lord bless you and keep you. The Lord make his face to shine on you and be gracious to you. The Lord look upon you with favor and give you peace.
C: Amen

HYMN "Precious Lord, Take My Hand"

Reprinted with permission from the Rev. Robert C. Barger from "Service of the Word and Prayer for the Columbine High School Community," Abiding Hope Lutheran Church, Littleton, Colorado, April 21, 1999.

A Service of Healing

PRELUDE

WELCOME

A CALL TO HEALING FOR THE HEALERS

Leader: Jesus asked, "Who proved neighbor to the one who fell among robbers?"
The Healers: They answered him, "The one who showed mercy on him."
Leader: "Go and do likewise," Jesus said.
The Healers: We come together as those who show mercy in need of mercy and renewal. We come carrying scars and wounds because we have loved.
Leader: Jesus said, "Whoever receives one such child in my name receives me."
The Healers: We come together mindful of all the children we serve. Their needs are so many and our resources are so limited.
Leader: Jesus also said, "As you did it to one of the least of these my brothers and sisters, you did it also to me."
The Healers: We come together mindful of the most vulnerable in our community: couples desperate for a child, children whom no one wants, the poor, the struggling, the aging, the refugees, the troubled and the tired. Their needs are so many and our resources are so few.
Leader: Jesus said, "Wherever two or three are gathered in my name, I am there in the midst of them."

The Healers: We come to experience God's peace and renewal in the Lord who went to the cross.

Leader: Thus, Jesus said, "Come unto me all who are weary and heavy laden and I will give you rest."

The Healers: We come to the Lord at this hour for the rest and renewal that only God can give!

HYMN: "Healer of Our Every Ill"

(Please sit.)

WORDS OF HEALING FROM THE PSALMS: Psalm 103 *(read responsively)*
[The text for these readings was provided to participants.]

FIRST LESSON: Isaiah 40:28-31

(Please stand.)

GOSPEL LESSON: John 21:1-17

(Please sit.)

HOMILY

(Please stand.)

HYMN: "You Who Dwell in the Shelter of the Lord" ("On Eagle's Wings")

(Please sit.)

AN ACT OF HEALING

You are invited to come forward and light a candle for a special person and to place it on the credence table. After lighting the candle, you may go to one of the pastors for anointing with oil and for a prayer of healing and renewal.

(Please stand.)

THE BIDDING PRAYERS

At the invitation of the pastor, you are invited to speak specific names or concerns.

Leader: Let us pray for those who receive our services and our ministry that they might know of God's presence through our presence.
For birth mothers in their struggles and decisions *(first names)*;
For adoptive parents as they prepare to receive children *(first names)*;
For young people and their counselors that wise decisions may be made *(first names)*;
For the aged in their loneliness, infirmity, or confusion *(first names)*;
For refugees and those who care for them as they make a new home *(first names)*;
And for all others who we serve that they may know of Christ's love through ours *(first names)*.
Lord of the vulnerable,
The Healers: Hear our prayer!
Leader: Let us pray for those who offer care, counsel, and resources through our agency that we and they may be strengthened for ministry.
For those who are tired through long hours of work *(silence)*;
For those who are worn down by endless red tape *(silence)*;
For those who efforts are rejected and ignored, resented and fought by the very ones they hope to serve *(silence)*;
For case workers, administrators, office personnel, and supervisors who battle frustration, fatigue, and cynicism *(silence)*;
And for our colleagues near and far who join us in our common concerns and often in our need for healing, especially *(first names)*.
Lord of the vulnerable,
The Healers: Hear our prayer!
Leader: The God who brought life to Jesus and the renewing Spirit to the church will give to us that which we need to do God's work. Hear the words of Paul: "Rejoice in the Lord always; again I say, Rejoice! Let all know of your patience. The Lord is near. Do not be anxious about anything, but in everything, by prayer and petition, with thanksgiving, present your request to God. And the peace of God which transcends all understanding, will guard you hearts and minds in Christ Jesus." Amen

THE LORD'S PRAYER

HYMN: "Precious Lord, Take My Hand"

THE SERENITY PRAYER
God, grant me the serenity
to accept the things I cannot change,
the courage to change the things I can,
and the wisdom to know the difference.
Living one day at a time,
enjoying one moment at a time;
accepting hardship as a pathway to peace;
taking, as Jesus did,
this sinful world as it is,
not as I would have it;
trusting that you will make all things right
if I surrender to your will;
so that I may be reasonably happy in this life
and supremely happy with you in the next. Amen

THE BENEDICTION
Leader: The Lord bless you and keep you. The Lord make his face to shine on you and to be gracious to you. The Lord look upon you with favor and give you peace.
The Healers: Amen

POSTLUDE

Reprinted from "A Service of Healing," Lutheran Family Services of Colorado. Held March 25, 1999, at Abiding Hope Lutheran Church, Littleton, Colorado. Used by permission.

NOTES

Introduction

    1. See Loren B. Mead, *The Once and Future Church: Reinventing the Congregation for a New Mission Frontier* (Washington, D.C.: Alban Institute, 1991).

    2. Marilyn Ferguson, *The Aquarian Conspiracy: Personal and Social Transformation in the 1980s* (Los Angeles: J. P. Tharcher, 1980), 72ff.

    3. William E. Hulme, *Managing Stress in Ministry* (San Francisco: Harper and Row Publishers, 1985), 22-24. I have adapted this Holmes/Rahe scale. See "Clergy Life Changes Rating Scale," in Clergy Self-Care: Finding a Balance (Washington, D.C.: Alban Institute, 1991), 30-31.

    4. William Bridges, *Managing Transitions: Making the Most Out of Change* (Reading, Mass.: Perseus Books, 1991), 3f.

    5. See Bridges, *Managing Transitions*, 5f.

    6. Bridges, *Managing Transitions*, 50.

    7. Cynthia D. Scott and Dennis T. Jaffe, *Managing Personal Change: A Primer for Today's World* (Los Altos, Calif.: Crisp Publications, 1989), 32.

    8. For a more extensive discussion, see Tom F. Driver, *Liberating Rites: Understanding the Transformative Power of Ritual* (Boulder, Colo.: Westview Press, 1998); and Cletus J. Wessels, *The Holy Web: The Church and the New Universe* (Maryknoll, N. Y.: Orbis Books, 2000).

Chapter 1

    1. See Tom F. Driver, *Liberating Rites: Understanding the Transformative Power of Ritual* (Boulder, Colo.: Westview Press, 1998), 13ff.

    2. Driver writes that we have tended to focus on "big" rituals such as "church services, funeral processions, state ceremonies, weddings, pilgrimages, festival, and the like" and separated them from the "little ones: acts of greeting and leave-taking, table manners, making beds, issuing invitations, going to Grandma's house, making a date, and so on. Ignoring these because of their daily familiarity, we do not notice how greatly our lives are affected by ritualizing activities that have become, as they are supposed to do, our 'second nature.'" *Liberating Rites*, 12f.

3. Driver, *Liberating Rites*, 12f.
4. Driver, *Liberating Rites*, 16f.
5. Bruce Reed, *The Dynamics of Religion: Process and Movement in Christian Churches* (London: Darton, Longman, and Todd, Ltd., 1978), 32.
6. "Tradition," in *Life According to Tony*, a six-part audiocassette series. Available from EAPE/Kingdomworks, Eastern College, 1300 Eagle Road, St. Davids, PA 19087; 610-341-1722.

Chapter 2
1. Eugene Roehlkepartain and Peter Benson, *Youth in Protestant Churches* (Minneapolis: Search Institute, 1993), 121-25; and Peter Benson, Eugene Roehlkepartain, and Shelby Andress, *Congregations at Crossroads* (Minneapolis: Search Institute, 1995), 21.
2. Mark Holman, "Home as First Church," *Lutheran Partners* (July/August 1997): 18f.
3. Peter Benson, in a presentation at "Faith Talks," a conference sponsored by Augsburg Youth and Family Institute, Augsburg College, Minneapolis, Minnesota, spring 1995.
4. William Bridges, *Transitions: Making Sense of Life's Changes* (Reading, Mass.: Addison-Wesley Publishing, 1980); and William Bridges, *Managing Transitions: Making the Most of Change* (Reading, Mass.: Perseus Books, 1991).
5. Gertrud Mueller Nelson, *To Dance with God: Family Ritual and Community Celebration* (New York: Paulist Press, 1986); Meg Cox, The Heart of a Family: Searching America for New Traditions that Fulfill Us (New York: Random House, 1998); and Tom F. Driver, *Liberating Rites: Understanding the Transformative Power of Rituals* (Boulder, Colo.: Westview Press, 1998).
6. Roy M. Oswald, "Gentle Loving God" and "Thy Care and Calm," *Chants for the Road*, audiocassette (Boonsboro, Md.: Life Structure Resources, 1991). Available from Life Structure Resources, 5658 Amos Reeder Rd., Boonsboro, MD 21713; 800-723-0625.
7. David Richards, "Support Systems," a paper distributed by the Office of Pastoral Development, Coral Gables, Fla., 1974; quoted in James Fenhagen, Mutual Ministry: New Vitality for the Local Church, (New York: Seabury Press, 1977), 101.

Chapter 3
1. Kent Nerburn, *Small Graces: The Quiet Gifts of Everyday Life* (Novato, Calif.: New World Library, 1998), 31.
2. Roy M. Oswald, *Fasting/Conscious Eating*, audiocassette (Boonsboro, Md.: Life Structure Resources, 1991). Available from Life Structure Resources, 5658 Amos Reeder Rd., Boonsboro, MD 21713; 800-723-0625.
3. Roy M. Oswald, *Body Stretches for Health and Vitality*, audiocassette.

(Boonsboro, Md.: Life Structure Resources, 1991). Available from Life Structure Resources, 5658 Amos Reeder Rd., Boonsboro, MD 21713; 800-723-0625.

4. Flora Slosson Wuellner, "Transformation: Our Fear, Our Longing," *Weavings* (March/April 1991): 10.

5. Roy M. Oswald, *Chants for the Road*, audiocassette (Boonsboro, Md.: Life Structure Resources, 1991). Available from Life Structure Resources, 5658 Amos Reeder Rd., Boonsboro, MD 21713; 800-723-0625.

6. Roy M. Oswald, "Clergy Burnout Rating Scales," *Clergy Self-Care: Finding a Balance* (Washington, D.C.: Alban Institute, 1991), 61-65.

7. These rituals were prepared by Catherine Malotky for her daughters, Cara (at age 12)) and Abbie (at age 11). See appendix D.

8. My thanks to Sandra Skach, St. Paul, Minnesota, and her family for allowing me to tell this story.

9. Watty Piper, ill. George and Doris Hauman, *The Little Engine That Could* (New York: Grosset & Dunlap, 1976).

10. Jean Morris Trumbauer, "Forty Days and Forty Nights: Diary of a Dream" (Minneapolis: 1997).

Chapter 4

1. William Bridges, *Transitions: Making Sense of Life's Changes* (Reading, Mass.: Addison-Wesley Publishing, 1980), 15.

2. See Carolyn Luetje and Meg Marcrander, *Face to Face with God in Your Home: Guiding Children and Youth in Prayer* (Minneapolis: Augsburg Fortress, 1995).

3. My thanks to Jean Giebenhain and Tim Berg for allowing me to share this story.

4. Jean and Tim and their daughters—Julie, Renu, and Susha—gave their permission for me to share this story. I thank them for their generosity!

5. "Called as Partners in Christ's Service," Jane Parker Huber, 1981; "Here I Am, Lord," Daniel Schutte, 1981; "We Are Called," David Haas, 1988.

6. For further resources, see the following: Elizabeth O'Connor, *Call to Commitment: The Story of the Church of The Saviour* (New York: Harper and Row, 1963); Ed White, *Lay Communique* 2, no. 4 (Fall 1995); Jean Morris Trumbauer, *Created and Called: Discovering Our Gifts for Abundant Living* (Minneapolis: Augsburg Fortress, 1998); Office of Enlistment Services, National Ministries, Presbyterian Church (U.S.A.)*This Call's for You: A Christian Vocation Workbook for Congregations—Leader's Guide* (Louisville, Ky.: Presbyterian Church [U.S.A.], 1993; and Carol L. Weiser, Sally Simmel, and Bob Sitze, *Working: Making a Difference in God's World*, ed. Carol L. Weiser (Chicago: Evangelical Lutheran Church in America, 1995).

7. John W. Arthur, 1972.

8. "Here I Am, Lord," Daniel Schutte, 1981; "O Christ, the Great Foundation,"

Timothy T'ingfang Lew, trans. Mildred A. Wiant, 1933; "Spirit, Spirit of Gentleness," James K. Manley, 1978; "Come, O Spirit, John A. Dalles, 1983; "Come, Great God of All the Ages," Mary Jackson Cathey, 1987; "Wind Who Makes All Winds that Called," Thomas H. Troeger, 1983; "Come, O Spirit, Dwell Among Us," Janie Alford, 1979; "Spirit of the Living God," Daniel Iverson, 1935; and "We Are Called," David Haas, 1988.

9. "Creative God, Your Fingers Trace," Jeffrey Rowthorn, 1979; "Morning Has Broken," Eleanor Farjeon, 1931; or "God, You Spin the Whirling Planets," Jane Parker Huber, 1978.

10. "Let Us Talents and Tongues Employ," Fred Kaan, 1975; "We Are All One in Mission," Rusty Edwards, 1986; and "You Are the Seed," Cesáreo Gabaraub, trans. Raquel Gutiérrez-Achon and Skinner Chávez-Melo, 1979.

11. Ed White, *Saying Goodbye* (Washington, D.C.: Alban Institute, 1990); Roy M. Oswald, *Running Through the Thistles* (Washington, D.C.: Alban Institute, 1984).

12. This was done at St. Albert the Great Catholic Parish in Minneapolis, Minnesota, in 1997.

13. Thanks to Speed Leas, senior consultant at the Alban Institute, for these suggestions.

14. For suggested sentence completion exercises to use as community building reflections at meetings, see Jean Morris Trumbauer, *Created and Called*, 58, 147f., 177 ff., and 188.

15. See Jean Morris Trumbauer, *Created and Called*, 221; or Roy D. Phillips, Letting Go: Energizing People for Ministry (Bethesda, Md.: Alban Institute, 1999).

16. "We Are Called," David Haas, 1988; "Lord, You Give the Great Commission," Jeffrey Rowthorn, 1978; and "Let Us Talents and Tongues Employ," Fred Kaan, 1975.

Chapter 5

1. "All Things Bright and Beautiful," Cecil Frances Alexander, 1848.

2. "The Earth Is Our Mother, We Must Take Care of Her," from the audiocassette *Circle the Earth with Song*. Chants sung by Susan Elizabeth Hale, Albuquerque, N.M.: Southwest Center for Music and Imagery, 1979. Available from Southwest Center for Music and Imagery, Box 4109, Albuquerque, NM 87196-4190.

3. James P. Wind, "Celebrating Congregations," in *Congregations: The Alban Journal* 25, no. 1 (January-February 1999): 3.

4. Ibid.

5. "Whatsoever You Do" (text: Matt. 5:3-12), Willard F. Jabusch, 1982.

6. "Gift of Finest Wheat," Omer Westendorf, 1976.

7. "Be Not Afraid" (based on Isaiah 42:2-3 and Luke 6:20ff.), Bob Dufford, S. J., 1975; and "O Healing River," Fran Minkoff, 1964.

8. I became aware of this song through my friend Lydia Walker, who first heard it during a sweat lodge experience conducted by an Apache tribe in Arizona.

She said that the song has been used for so long that no one knows its origins; people just pass it along and give it away.

9. "O God, Our Help in Ages Past," Isaac Watts, 1719.

10. "Michael, Row the Boat Ashore," traditional Caribbean folk song.

11. These prayer vigils are sponsored by the Church Federation of Greater Indianapolis, 317-926- 5371. The vigils were begun in February 1996. Vigils have been held in memory of over 550 people. The Sanctuary Church Movement is under the direction of the federation.

12. Edward J. Hayes, *The Little Tin Box*. Available from Videos with Values, 5901 West Main, Suite A, Belleville, IL 62223; 618-235-8700. 30 minutes.

13. From the Silent Witness National Initiative vision statement and web site: http://www.silentwitness.net/html/swni.html

14. This ritual was developed by members of Eastshore Unitarian Universalist Church in Kirtland, Ohio.

15. Shortly after the bombing of the Federal Building in Oklahoma City, Oklahoma, in April 1995, Gary Harbaugh, a member of of the Lutheran Disaster Response Team sponsored by the Evangelical Lutheran Church in America, presented an address in that community. Two years later, none of the 27 clergy who had attended Harbaugh's workshop was still serving a congregation in that community. Many left for other positions; some died of heart attacks; others were divorced and then moved.

Chapter 6

1. See Charles J. Keating, *Who We Are Is How We Pray: Matching Personality and Spirituality* (Mystic, Conn.: Twenty-Third Publications, 1987); Malcolm Goldsmith, *Knowing Me Knowing God: Exploring Your Spirituality with Myers-Briggs* (Nashville: Abingdon Press, 1997); Chester P. Michael and Marie C. Norrisey, *Prayer and Temperament* (Charlottesville, Va.: Open Door, 1985); Lynne M. Baab, *Personality Type in Congregations* (Bethesda, Md.: Alban Institute, 1998); and Jean Morris Trumbauer, *The Learning Styles Inventory in Faith Communities: A Facilitator's Guide* (Plymouth, Minn.: Personal Power Products, 1998).

2. Eleanor S. Corlett and Nancy B. Millner, *Navigating Midlife: Using Typology as a Guide* (Palo Alto, Calif.: Consulting Psychologists Press Books, 1993), 7, quoted in Lynne M. Baab, *Personality Type in Congregations* (Bethesda, Md.: Alban Institute, 1998), 30.

3. Kathleen Fischer, *Women at the Well: Feminist Perspectives on Spiritual Direction* (New York: Paulist Press, 1988), 113.

4. Categories and conceptual model drawn from Evan Imber-Black and Janine Roberts, *Rituals for Our Times* (New York: Harper Collins, 1992), 58-73.

5. See David L. Miller, "Creating Rituals," *The Lutheran*, July 1999, 13; and Renee Beck and Sydney Barbara Metrick, *The Art of Ritual: A Guide to Creating and Performing Your Own Ceremonies for Growth and Change* (Berkeley, Calif.: Celestial Arts, 1990), 87-90, 93-105.

ANNOTATED BILIOGRAPHY

Anderson, Herbert, and Edward Foley. *Mighty Stories, Dangerous Rituals: Weaving Together the Human and the Divine*. San Francisco: Jossey-Bass, 1998.

Describes how special ceremonies such as baptisms, weddings, and funerals can be more meaningful and transformative when those involved offer personal stories as part of the ritual.

Beck, Renee, and Sydney Barbara Metrick. *The Art of Ritual: A Guide to Creating and Performing Your Own Ceremonies for Growth and Change*. Berkeley, Calif.: Celestial Arts, 1990.

Engaging book on ritual, its purposes, history, symbols, and processes. Provides helpful guidelines and work sheets for special applications to individuals, families, and groups.

Bridges, William. *Managing Transitions: Making the Most Out of Change*. Reading, Mass.: Perseus Books, 1991.

Excellent resource on dealing with corporate change and assisting both managers and employees through the stages of workplace transition in ways that minimize disruptions and human breakage.

———. *Transitions: Making Sense of Life's Changes*. Reading, Mass.: Addison-Wesley Publishing, 1980.

Easy-to-understand, classic work on transition processes in our lives. Lays out this basic theory of the three stages of transitions—endings, the neutral zones, and new beginnings—and provides strategies for each stage.

Conlon, James A. *Lyrics for Re-Creation: Language for the Music of the Universe*. New York: Continuum Publishing Co., 1997.

A powerfully moving book for all who love life on this earth. Helpful discussion questions and suggestions for ritual and other actions that move one from reflection to action on behalf of the earth and humanity.

Cox, Meg, *The Heart of a Family: Searching America for New Traditions that Fulfill Us.* New York: Random House, 1998.

An excellent resource for family ritual. Addresses events from grand holiday celebrations to everyday bedtime routines and why they have a lasting impact on children, their identities, and transitions.

Driver, Tom F. *Liberating Rites: Understanding the Transformative Power of Ritual.* Boulder, Colo.: Westview Press, 1998.

An engaging and thorough scholarly work on ritual and its transformative power in our lives. Examination of the central role of ritual in all living beings and its contribution to order, security, religious beliefs, and the formation of human community.

Hammerschlag, Carl A., and Howard D. Silverman. *Healing Ceremonies: Creating Personal Rituals for Spiritual, Emotional, Physical, and Mental Health.* New York: Perigee Book, Berkley Publishing Group, 1997.

The physician-authors share stories about those who have confronted illness with personal ceremony and ritual and offer simple guidelines for creating rituals for ourselves that strengthen our mind, body, and spirit

Hays, Edward M. *Prayers for the Domestic Church: A Handbook for Worship in the Home.* Leavenworth, Kan.: Forest of Peace Publishing, 1979.

Companion prayer book to Hays's Prayers for Planetary Christians, this book provides over 120 ritual prayers and blessings for a wide spectrum of situations in daily life.

Imber-Black, Evan, and Janine Roberts. *Rituals for Our Times.* New York: Harper Collins, 1992.

A comprehensive review of ritual processes and how they mark transitions, express essential values, provide healing, and deepen relationships. Authors address how gender roles are reflected in ritual and how revitalized traditions can alter the course of intimate relationships.

Luetje, Carolyn, and Meg Marcrander. *Face to Face with God in Your Home: Guiding Children and Youth in Prayer.* Minneapolis: Augsburg Fortress, 1995.

Excellent guidebook to assist church leaders and parents to pray with children. Provides basic age-level developmental information, activity sheets, and suggested further resources.

Nelson, Gertrud Mueller. *To Dance with God: Family Ritual and Community Celebration.* New York: Paulist Press, 1986.

Author addresses the history, psychology, and spirituality of ritual. She suggests a number of rituals for families with young children.

Oswald, Roy M. *Body Stretches for Health and Vitality*, audiocassette. Boonsboro, Md.: Life Structure Resources, 1991. Available from Life Structure Resources, 5658 Amos Reeder Rd., Boonsboro, MD 21713; 800-723-0625.

Teaches Hatha Yoga muscle stretches to keep your body loose and limber. When used daily, the stretches become a meditation of movement.

————. *Chants for the Road*, audiocassette. Boonsboro, Md.: Life Structure Resources, 1991. Available from Life Structure Resources, 5658 Amos Reeder Rd., Boonsboro, MD 21713; 800-723-0625.

A dozen of Roy Oswald's favorite chants to use while driving. The introduction suggests why chants can change a driver's disposition and identity on the road.

————. *Fasting/Conscious Eating*, audiocassette. Boonsboro, Md.: Life Structure Resources, 1991. Available from Life Structure Resources, 5658 Amos Reeder Rd., Boonsboro, MD 21713; 800-723-0625.

Oswald explains the spiritual discipline of fasting and how going without food makes us aware of our spiritual hunger. Discusses ways to be a conscious eater who ingests food with new awareness of self and the Holy.

Trumbauer, Jean Morris. *Created and Called: Discovering Our Gifts for Abundant Living*. Minneapolis: Augsburg Fortress, 1998.

A manual providing numerous ways for members to discover their personal giftedness. Many ideas suitable for rituals at the beginning or conclusion of group meetings in the church and a dozen rituals to use for celebrating lay ministry or personal gifts-discovery.

Weiser, Carol L., Sally Simmel, and Bob Sitze. Edited by Carol L. Weiser. *Working: Making a Difference in God's World*. Chicago: Evangelical Lutheran Church in America, 1995.

Hands-on resource book to help congregational leaders equip their members for ministry in daily life in the workplace. Includes models, stories, programs, and practical ideas to get any church started in this essential support for ministry in the marketplace.

Torvend, Samuel, ed. *Welcome Home: Scripture, Prayers and Blessings for the Household*. Minneapolis: Augsburg Fortress, 1995.

A series of three books, one for each liturgical year, organized according to the Sundays and seasons of the church year. Includes a new daily lectionary, prayers for work and home, psalms and texts, and special prayers for use throughout the day.